PROMOTING

ISSUES

&IDEAS

2ND EDITION

A GUIDE TO PUBLIC RELATIONS
FOR NONPROFIT ORGANIZATIONS

PROMOTING

ISSUES & IDEAS

2ND EDITION

A GUIDE TO PUBLIC RELATIONS FOR NONPROFIT ORGANIZATIONS

by M Booth & Associates, Inc.

The Foundation Center • 1995

Library of Congress Cataloging-in-Publication Data

Promoting issues & ideas: a guide to public relations for nonprofit
   organizations / by M Booth & Associates, Inc. — [Rev. ed.]
      p.   cm.
   Includes bibliographical references and index.
   ISBN 0-87954-594-1
   1. Nonprofit organizations—Management. 2. Public relations.
I. M Booth & Associates.   II. Title: Promoting issues and ideas.
HD62.6.P76M   1995
659.2'88—dc20   94-45862
                                            CIP

Dedicated to Bill Ruder

M Booth & Associates

M Booth & Associates is one of the nation's leading communications firms and has a long history of promoting issues and ideas in the public affairs and nonprofit arenas.

Founded in 1976 as an agency whose focus was on helping nonprofit organizations and institutions, it now specializes in marketing and corporate communications, public affairs, business-to-business and health-care public relations.

M Booth & Associates has helped hundreds of educational, philanthropic, cultural, and social-service organizations communicate better through creative public relations campaigns—from galvanizing public opinion on issues such as hunger, women's rights, and racial justice, to recruiting volunteers to tutor in New York City's public schools, to promoting national public-policy awards for innovative state and local government programs, to building audiences for public television programming.

Named as one of the "best managed" and "most strategic" firms in consecutive years by the leading industry publication, M Booth has received public relations' highest awards for its design, writing, and creativity, and has been recognized as a champion of nonprofit organizations nationwide.

Headquartered in New York City, the agency operates BoothNet, a network of 13 affiliate public relations firms located throughout the United States, and is a member of Proclaim, an international group of 17 public relations agencies located throughout the United Kingdom, Europe, and Australia.

Contents

Acknowledgments

This second edition of *Promoting Issues and Ideas* was revised with the invaluable advice and contributions of many people. Our thanks to the M Booth & Associates staff, especially Janet Bartucci, Karen Borack, Patricia Browne, Jane Cabot, Patricia Garrison, Raina Grossman, and Emily Whitfield for their expertise and writing; Ken Ulmer for his thorough research; and Lidell Jackson for again producing a perfect manuscript. Most of all, special thanks to Elizabeth Chute for serving as editor, keeping us on deadline, and turning out a book we're proud to publish.

We would also like to express our gratitude to Elizabeth McCormack, Chairman, M Booth & Associates, for her support and guidance throughout our 18-year history.

Margaret Booth
President

Brad Rodney
Managing Partner

Foreword

". . . If the circus is coming to town and you paint a sign saying 'Circus Coming to the Fairground Saturday' that's advertising. If you put the sign on the back of an elephant and walk it into town, that's promotion. If the elephant walks through the mayor's flower bed, that's publicity. And if you can get the mayor to laugh about it, that's public relations."
—Reader's Digest

Public relations may seem a uniquely 20th-century activity. Actually, it's been around ever since ancient storytellers chronicled the exploits of their warrior chiefs—no doubt embellishing their heroics and minimizing their flaws along the way.

Public relations as we know it today has changed radically in recent years. Rapid advances in information technology have made it possible to communicate in ways not even dreamed of ten years ago. In this new information age, we're bombarded daily with thousands of messages via fax, computer, and dozens of TV and cable TV channels.

The revolution in communications has significantly altered trends in the American workplace as well. According to one estimate, two-thirds of all jobs in the U.S. are "information related"—and that number is bound to grow as the economy continues to shift toward service industries and away from manufacturing jobs.

As the explosion of information technology has enabled us to communicate more quickly and effectively, public relations has taken on a broader role as support for successful marketing and sales efforts in businesses of all sizes. In order to distinguish themselves from the competition and improve their bottom lines, corporations spend hundreds of millions of "PR dollars" each year to promote themselves, their chief executives, their products and services, and their corporate good works.

Nonprofit organizations may not need to sell products, but in this age of sophisticated communication strategies and competing messages they do need to sell themselves, their ideas, and their services. In order to survive—even more, to thrive—nonprofits must establish their own individual niche in the crowded marketplace of ideas.

In the simplest terms, public relations is letting others know about you. It may be as straightforward as attracting an audience to a museum exhibit or finding volunteers for a literacy program. It can be as complicated as influencing a public-policy issue or increasing the awareness of an organization among potential funders.

Since our founding in 1976 as a public-affairs agency, M Booth & Associates has counseled all kinds of organizations—large and small—on how to use public relations to:

- build credibility
- develop institutional awareness
- change the public's perception of an organization
- advocate for change
- promote a name change
- defuse crises
- create coalitions
- increase membership
- publicize research findings
- promote events and milestones
- support fundraising campaigns

Nonprofit organizations often believe their programs will sell themselves. Nothing could be further from the truth. Even the best of programs will fade into obscurity unless those who need to know about them are made aware. Imagine, for example, that a community organization is announcing grants to provide health services for women in traditionally underserved neighborhoods but forgets to invite community-based media to its press conference. As obvious as that error may seem, it can occur when an organization believes that support and recognition will come naturally to a good cause.

No nonprofit organization is too small to benefit from a public relations campaign. And while size obviously has something to do with how much money can be spent, every organization can plan a public relations effort designed to accommodate the limitations of a budget.

This book attempts to help nonprofits better manage and carry out a public relations program. For the incipient organization, we hope it serves as an invaluable guide to planning and executing a public relations effort. For those organizations more experienced in public relations, the book can be used as a handy reference when developing strategies or implementing new ideas.

Regardless of an organization's size or objective, we believe several elements must be in place before it can launch a successful public relations program:

- The organization must know what it is. That means it must have specifically defined goals and objectives.

- These goals and objectives must be articulated clearly by both staff and board in the same way. The staff cannot describe the organization in one manner and the board describe it in another.

- Public relations thinking should be a part of the organization's strategic planning. Public relations must be an integral part of management and be given a prominent role in the organization. The staff member responsible for public relations should have direct access to the chief executive, who must consider PR among the organization's top priorities.

- An organization must know who it wants to reach and why. In other words, it must be able to identify those audiences key to its survival.

- An organization must have a public relations plan—a strategy for carrying out its PR program. Such a plan is an effective tool for keeping the process on track and provides an important means of evaluation at the completion of the program.

- An organization must have a public relations budget, even if it is minuscule, so that a plan can be crafted that makes sense given the dollars available.

- The public relations plan must generate consensus. Everyone in the organization must believe in it and stand behind it.

- The organization must understand that public relations offers no quick fix. It takes time to build visibility and/or change perceptions. Public relations doesn't work overnight.

- Public relations cannot substitute for substance. If an organization lacks a real program, public relations won't work.

This book is organized from a public relations planner's point of view. It starts with the planning process and then provides in-depth information on how to use the tools—publicity campaigns, printed materials, new communications technologies, etc. We've tried to provide as many actual examples and case studies as possible. If time is a problem, a good deal of information and insight can be gained by reading selected chapters.

Whatever your approach, we invite your comments so that we can learn from your experiences as well.

The staff of M Booth & Associates

1   The Public Relations Plan

A public relations plan is the road map of public relations activity undertaken by an organization.

Usually, plans are organized for both the short and long term. Most often they are developed to encompass a period of three to five years. Realistically, this means that goals and objectives are developed over the long term, while specific activities are detailed for a shorter period (usually a year). For this reason, a public relations plan should be updated annually so that it reflects the changing needs of an organization. At the same time, it should be applied on a daily or weekly basis to ensure that the public relations program is on track.

Because public relations is so hard to quantify—for example, it's often impossible to measure to what extent newspaper publicity resulted in increased funds—the public relations plan can serve as an important tool for evaluating whether an organization's objectives are being met successfully.

All public relations plans should consist of the following elements:

1. *Objectives—What does the organization want the plan to accomplish?* Objectives should be straightforward and clearly stated. For an arts organization this could be "to increase audiences"; for a civil-rights group, "to rally public

"... *What are the one or two most important ideas the organization wishes to communicate to its audiences?*"

support around an issue"; for a day-care center, "to obtain more clients."

Most plans have more than one objective, depending on the kind and number of audiences to be reached.

2. *Target audiences—Whom must the organization reach or influence to make the program work?* Like objectives, most groups have multiple audiences with whom they must communicate. These audiences usually include both internal and external groups of people.

The term *internal audience* refers to those groups closest to the organization, including but not necessarily limited to the staff and board. Often, especially if it is a national organization, it will include a broader group such as chapter presidents.

External audience refers to targeted groups independent of the organization. For a day-care center, for example, these might include working mothers, principals, school supervisors, teachers, funders, government officials in the day-care area, and staff at other day-care centers.

When identifying audiences, it is critical that you determine priorities so that the public relations program reflects the appropriate emphasis. In the case of the day-care center, working mothers and funders are probably more important audiences than teachers, for without their knowledge and support the center could not survive.

3. *Key messages—What are the one or two most important ideas the organization wishes to communicate to its audiences?* In the case of the day-care center, the key messages might be as basic as "We care for your child as carefully as you would" or "High-quality day care is crucial to every child's development." The spirit of the key messages should permeate the public relations plan—and written materials—of any organization, as well as reflect a consensus with which the entire organization is comfortable.

4. *Strategies—What grand design or overall approach should the organization adopt to reach its targeted audiences?* A common strategy adopted by many organizations is to use media relations to heighten institutional awareness. Other strategies might include expanding outreach efforts to increase the number of volunteers, or creating a special event to launch a fundraising campaign or draw attention to an important issue.

5. *Tactics—What tools should the organization employ to carry out its strategies?* It could be a simple publicity cam-

paign, new print or multimedia materials, a special event, an awards program, institutional advertising—or all of the above (see Example 1).

6. *Timetable—What is a realistic time period for developing and carrying out the strategies the organization plans to adopt?* Timetables are usually organized by the year and month, but attention should also be given to daily and weekly scheduling of projects.

7. *Budget—What should the size and scope of the organization's public relations program be?* It depends on the amount of money available. It is better to plan broadly and then weigh choices against budget constraints and the potential effectiveness of a particular strategy. Details about how to budget follow later in this chapter.

EXAMPLE 1.   Sample Strategies and Tactics for Reaching the Target Audience

Group	Objective	Audience	Strategy	Tactic
Performing-arts organization	Increase credibility of organization	Theatergoers Funders	Use media relations to increase awareness; create new special event	Newspaper reviews; special free performance and party
Day-care center	Attract more clients	Parents Teachers Principals	Media relations; special event	Local publicity; newsletter; special conference
Civil rights organization	Gain legislative support for an issue	Voters Lawmakers	Media relations; expand outreach efforts	National publicity (news and editorial coverage); letter-writing campaign

A PUBLIC RELATIONS PLAN—ARTS APPRECIATION FOR CHILDREN

The following is an example of a public relations plan developed for a client, which we'll call Arts Appreciation for Children (AAFC). The plan's elements can be adopted for use by organizations of any size (see Example 2).

"Note that some of the objectives are long range, while others can be accomplished more quickly. . . ."

Arts Appreciation for Children is a community organization that seeks to improve children's appreciation of art. It believes in exposing children to contemporary artists and live performances and would like all schools in the area to adopt this teaching approach. However, since art appreciation is not considered as important as reading or math, AAFC must battle to change that perception.

Public Relations Objectives

The following objectives have been developed to change and strengthen perceptions of AAFC and its issue—arts appreciation. Note that some of the objectives are long range, while others can be accomplished more quickly:

- to bring the courses, workshops, and resources of AAFC to the attention of teachers, parents, volunteers, schools, and organizations that can benefit from them (short range)
- to bring the activities and accomplishments of AAFC to the attention of potential donors and members (short range)
- to establish, as an educational issue, the importance of children learning to appreciate the arts (long range)
- to encourage teachers' colleges to incorporate training in the use of arts appreciation into their curricula (long range)

EXAMPLE 2.   Plan Summary: Arts Appreciation for Children

Objective	Audience	Strategy	Tactic
Short Range			
Bring AAFC courses, workshops to the attention of potential attendees	Private and public school principals and teachers; parents; community, professional, and parent groups	Develop new materials, use media relations to increase awareness, expand community outreach	Tagline, news releases, public service announcements, advertising, direct-mail announcements, posters

EXAMPLE 2.   Plan Summary: Arts Appreciation for Children

Objective	Audience	Strategy	Tactic
Bring AAFC activities and accomplishments to attention of donors and members	Above groups, foundation and corporate philanthropy administrators, general public	New materials, media relations, expand outreach, special events	Tagline, media tour, news releases, PSAs, brochure series, institutional advertising, direct-mail offer, awards dinner
Long Range			
Establish the need for AAFC-advocated teaching methods as an issue	Teachers' college officials and professors, board of education members, school boards, teachers' groups, education administrators, parents	New materials, media relations	Issue kit, media tour, bylined articles, op-ed pieces, meetings with editorial boards, brochure series, survey, institutional advertising
Encourage teachers' colleges to teach AAFC-advocated instructional methods	Teachers' college officials, professional and educational organizations	Media relations, new materials, expand outreach	Bylined articles, brochure series, survey, institutional advertising, meetings with curricula planning boards

Audiences

AAFC's communications program is targeted to different population groups. A breakdown of these groups will help in identifying the specific messages that must be shaped as well as in selecting the appropriate media for reaching those audiences.

Target audiences for AAFC include the following:

- education professionals—teachers' college officials and professors, private and public school principals and teachers (nursery through high school)
- volunteers who teach arts appreciation to school children or adults
- parents of preschool and school-age children
- community, professional, and parent organizations
- donors and potential donors (includes all of the above)

"As the first words a reader . . . associates with the organization, the tagline is an important step in establishing an organizational identity."

First-Year Recommendations

Below are a number of recommendations AAFC will consider when shaping its public relations program. The tactics reflect the program's objectives, audiences, and strategies.

Tagline. (This particular tactic is designed to clearly articulate the group's purpose.) In just a few words, a tagline begins to tell the AAFC story before any of the communications materials on which it might appear—before the news release, before the brochure, etc. As the first words a reader of AAFC materials associates with the organization, the tagline is an important step in establishing an organizational identity.

To be most effective, the tagline should be incorporated into AAFC's logo and used on all materials distributed by the organization, including media kits, newsletters, stationery, program announcements, and fundraising appeals.

AAFC's tagline should be informative to both those familiar and unfamiliar with the organization. It should have relevance to all the target audiences cited above.

Arts Appreciation Issue Kit. (Here media are being used as a strategy, not as an audience.) The issues that AAFC is concerned with need to be outlined and shaped for the media. While some reporters may have a good understanding of the general issues, it is still necessary to provide them with information from AAFC's viewpoint. Written material that puts the organization's policies in simple language is often helpful to a reporter writing for a general audience.

To define the concerns of AAFC, an *issue kit* should be prepared. Its purpose is to:

- introduce the media to AAFC and its policies
- encourage feature articles
- provide a basis for interviews with media contacts and editorial boards
- serve as background for news releases

In addition to exploring the importance of the arts in school curricula, the kit might also contain information on the scarcity of good arts programs in the nation's public schools. A vivid description of the problem will serve as a useful backdrop for AAFC's concerns. It will, by inference, state the case for expanded arts education in public schools.

Last but not least, the kit should also contain background information on the organization itself and its activities. The contents might include the following:

- a fact sheet on arts and education
- a backgrounder or Q&A on different methods of teaching arts appreciation to children
- a bylined op-ed article
- a list of books and teaching materials on arts appreciation, including where they are being taught and used
- a profile of AAFC
- a preprinted Rolodex card with AAFC's tagline, address, telephone number, and contact names
- AAFC brochures, program notices, and other materials

The kit should be distributed to education, culture, and social-issue reporters, editorial-page editors and editorial departments at broadcast media, writers and editors at news magazines and education trade publications, syndicated columnists, and freelance education writers and reporters.

Metropolitan Area Media Tour. (The media tour is one tactic for reaching parents and teachers.) Interviews on television and radio talk programs have been successful in generating interest in and inquiries about AAFC and its programs and services. Efforts to obtain such interviews should be continued and expanded.

The media outlets in a given community are finite, however, and included in that number are many which appeal to audiences that aren't targeted by the organization. For this reason, and because Arts Appreciation for Children serves teachers in the metropolitan area, we recommend seeking interviews with media in nearby areas.

Telephone interviews may be used to cut down on travel time and expenses, and where an in-studio taping is necessary it may be possible to schedule interviews with other media outlets and reporters in the area. A geographical limit corresponding to a reasonable commuting distance for teachers who wish to take advantage of the services promoted should be set, however.

Similarly, interviews and meetings should be sought with reporters and the editorial boards of local newspapers. The issue kit should serve as a focal point for discussion; the aim of such meetings is to generate an article or editorial reflecting the information and viewpoints laid out in the kit.

News Release Series. (This is another example of using the media to establish the organization's credibility.) Arts Appreciation for Children should routinely release information on its activities, workshops, and

"The issue kit should serve as a focal point for discussion. . . ."

". . . service-oriented releases may be more effective than news releases because of the value they hold for the reader."

programs to the media as far in advance of each event as possible. The advance notice is needed to encourage pre-event publicity, where appropriate, and enables reporters to note these events on their calendars. For major activities, a *reminder mailing* should be issued closer to the actual date.

Publicity for AAFC issues may also be obtained through the distribution of *service-oriented news releases*. These are not about the organization per se, but provide information on the teaching of reading that is useful to targeted audiences. The purpose of such releases is twofold:

- to attract attention to the methods advocated by AAFC
- to establish AAFC with the media as an authority on the teaching of arts appreciation to children

Although they're a less direct means of generating publicity, service-oriented releases may be more effective than news releases because of the value they hold for the reader. They also lend themselves to feature articles.

Arts Appreciation for Children should be credited throughout these releases as the source of the information provided, and wherever possible tie-ins should be made to its services and activities.

Examples of topics for service-oriented releases include:

- the best texts and materials for teaching arts appreciation
- successful arts-appreciation courses in schools
- schools and after-school programs where arts appreciation is taught
- new developments in teaching methods
- unusual or unique arts-appreciation programs
- volunteer programs in arts appreciation for children

Although service releases should be written with a specific audience in mind, a single topic can be modified and aimed toward several target groups. For example, a release providing tips for parents on teaching their children about the arts could also be sent to appropriate consumer publications. Trade periodicals in the field might be sent a similar release promoting the same tips and methods as a means of increasing student interest in the arts.

Finally, service-oriented releases should not contain dated material—though they can be made more effective by timing their distribution with specific events on the school calendar, such as the start of classes or the filing date for college applications.

Public-Service Announcements. (PSAs should complement, not re-place, other media efforts.) When thinking about a PSA campaign, it is important to distinguish between radio and television.

The simplicity and relatively low cost of radio PSAs make them an ideal vehicle for advertising programs offered by Arts Appreciation for Children. Their simplicity and affordability are also good reasons why PSAs should be used to supplement paid advertising and direct mail. Used by local broadcast media, PSAs will reach a composite audience of teachers, parents, volunteers, and community activists.

Although PSAs can be elaborate productions akin to commercial broadcast announcements, it is also possible to achieve substantial air-time through the distribution of PSA scripts—*live copy*—for announcers to read. Almost all radio stations use this format; some television stations use it as well, along with accompanying slides as visuals.

Every PSA script mailed to a station's public-affairs director should include 60-, 30- and 10-second versions. The more formats offered, the greater the likelihood an announcement will be used. New scripts and slides should be distributed every three to four months—again, variety and freshness will increase the chances of an announcement being used.

In addition to being relatively inexpensive, live-copy PSAs can also be produced and distributed quickly. This makes them ideal for promoting upcoming seminars and workshops, such as AAFC's annual teachers' conference. It should be noted, however, that radio stations often require copy several weeks in advance of airtime. Obviously, an announcement that does not date quickly—i.e., that is not tied to a specific event—will have a longer shelf life.

AAFC should test several types of public-service announcements to determine the kind of appeal that works best for the organization. These might include:

- a generic announcement describing the organization and its mission
- a membership appeal directed at teachers and parents
- an announcement (omitting specific dates and times) of ongoing programs and workshops
- an announcement of a specific event, such as the annual teachers' conference

Lastly, all public-service announcements should include a request for listener inquiries.

Videotaped and audiotaped PSAs, which give Arts Appreciation for Children complete control over the delivery of the message, are another option. For example, AAFC might want to use a celebrity in a PSA to attract greater attention and generate instant recognition. Even though

"Their simplicity and affordability are also good reasons why PSAs should be used to supplement paid advertising and direct mail."

*"The
brochures . . .
can serve both
as a means
of direct
communication
with . . . target
audiences and
as a vehicle for
publicity."*

audiences may not have heard of AAFC, they will often respond to a familiar personality. Taped productions are significantly more expensive than distribution of live copy, however, and may not warrant the added expense.

A word about television PSAs: the explosion of cable has vastly increased the number of potential outlets for public-service announcements. At the same time, public-service directors at TV stations are inundated with videotapes from every sort of worthy cause. As a result, only a relatively small number are actually shown, and few PSAs are aired during prime viewing time. In fact, many end up on the air late at night or in the wee hours of the morning.

When approaching a station about a PSA, an organization should first call to ascertain the name of the current public-service director and the videotape format required. The videotape should then be sent to the station along with a brief pitch letter summarizing its appeal, a transcript of its contents, and a copy of the organization's 501(c)(3) tax-exempt certificate. Relevant brochures may also be included.

Brochure Series. As a way of elaborating on certain positions concerning the teaching of arts appreciation, AAFC might consider producing a series of brochures, to be distributed via direct mail to members, donors, government and education officials, and deans and department heads at teachers' colleges; and offered to the general public through the media.

The brochures, designed as threefold pamphlets, can serve both as a means of direct communication with AAFC's target audiences and as a vehicle for publicity. They should be mailed to education reporters and consumer columnists accompanied by a release summarizing their content and announcing their availability to the general public. Each brochure should include a coupon that makes it easy for readers to request additional information on Arts Appreciation for Children, to apply for membership, and/or to declare a contribution. To ascertain the source of their interest in AAFC, you should ask those responding to the coupon to state their occupation.

Topics for the pamphlets, which should be issued two or three times a year, might include the following:

- Why Children Love the Arts
- How I Learned to Appreciate the Arts (by a famous artist)
- Arts Appreciation Programs in High Schools

Special Projects

A portion of the AAFC plan should be designed as a project "wish list," time and money permitting. Such a list might include a survey, institutional advertising, a special membership offer, and/or a special event celebrating arts appreciation in the public schools.

Survey. To gain a greater understanding of how the teaching of arts appreciation is viewed, AAFC might undertake a survey of teachers and parents in the area.

Institutional Advertising. Arts Appreciation for Children already advertises its programs in newspapers and trade publications. This approach should be broadened to draw attention to the organization itself, with ads directed at both potential donors and members.

Institutional advertising should promote the goals and policies of Arts Appreciation for Children and, at the same time, generate excitement in the reader. Although the ads should make an appeal for funds, their primary thrust should be to elicit interest in arts appreciation. Teachers should want to learn more about AAFC programs, and parents should want to know why their children are not being taught arts appreciation in school and what they can do to change the situation.

Membership Offer. Institutional advertising and direct-mail efforts designed to attract new members might include a special membership offer. The offer need not be elaborate, but it should promise something of value to the prospective member and it should be related intrinsically to Arts Appreciation for Children.

In addition to regular newsletters, program alerts, and an invitation to the annual conference, a membership package might also include a "Teacher-Parent Guide to Teaching Arts Appreciation." The cost of producing such a *premium* could be covered by raising the membership price marginally as well as by offering the premium to the public.

The cost and labor involved in preparing a premium may also be offset by its value as a publicity tool, since its content and availability can be promoted through news releases and PSAs.

Learning to Enjoy the Arts: A Celebration. Appreciating the visual and performing arts is an important value in most cultures, and some cultures attach special significance to it. There is an old custom that associates honey with a child's first experience with art in order to connect sweetness with beauty. Many people have fond reminiscences of their first concert or play.

"Institutional advertising and direct-mail efforts designed to attract new members might include a special membership offer."

Arts Appreciation for Children might stage a special fundraising event at which such memories are shared with the audience by a lineup of celebrities. Both personal and cultural stories could be told.

Teacher Achievement Awards. Arts Appreciation for Children should consider giving awards to teachers who are esteemed for their classroom teaching methods and/or their effectiveness in using special techniques to help children appreciate the arts. Awards could be given in specific categories—for example, preschool and kindergarten, elementary school, junior high school, high school, and adult.

THE PUBLIC RELATIONS AUDIT

From time to time, organizations that have had ongoing public relations programs may want to evaluate their efforts in an objective and detailed fashion before developing a new plan or continuing with the old one. Such an evaluation is called an audit, and its purpose is to survey the strengths and weaknesses of existing communications programs and personnel. An audit should answer certain key questions:

1. How is the organization currently perceived by its key audiences?
2. Is there a difference in perception between what an organization wants an audience to believe and what the audience actually believes?
3. Are the organization's publicity materials effective communications tools? Do they accurately reflect the communications objectives of the organization?
4. Are the personnel involved in the public relations effort doing an effective job?
5. In short, are the organization's communications strategies working effectively?

Uncovering the answers to these questions requires a great deal of management input, and indeed any audit should be conducted in conjunction with top management. Perhaps an ancillary group of board members, key volunteers, and selected staff might be formed as a sounding board for such a review.

The audit should consist of interviews (preferably face-to-face) with representatives of the organization's key internal and external audiences. These usually include board, staff, media, and donors. Then, depending

". . . any audit should be conducted in conjunction with top management."

on what kind of organization it is, the list may be extended to include users of a service, government officials, program clients, and so on.

A carefully developed questionnaire should be created for use during the interviews. The interviewer should ask the interviewee about his or her knowledge and perceptions of the organization, its public relations materials, and its staff. Among the basic questions usually included in an audit are:

1. How would you describe _____ (name of organization)?
2. What are its major programs?
3. Have you seen its materials? Which ones? Do you feel they effectively communicate the organization's objectives?
4. Have you read or heard about _____ (name of organization)? Where?
5. Are you aware of any new programs the organization has initiated recently?

These questions are usually supplemented by others that probe the interviewee's perceptions of the organization in terms of staff and specific programs.

From an analysis of the questionnaires, a clear picture detailing the strengths and weaknesses of the current public relations program eventually will emerge. This, in turn, will enable the organization to develop a well-thought-out plan to strengthen or expand its present efforts.

In general, a public relations audit performed by individuals belonging to an organization will cost less than one performed by an outside consultant. Often, however, someone from the outside—someone who is objective and can walk away from his or her recommendations—is in the best position to conduct an audit. This is particularly true when personnel changes may be needed or major shifts in budget allocations are warranted.

The following examples suggest the scope and purpose of a public relations audit:

1. A voluntary hospital and medical center, known throughout the area as a leading research and patient-care facility, seemed to be floundering while neighboring hospitals— smaller hospitals with far less impressive staffs, facilities, or research credentials—were garnering a great deal of attention and support. The hospital had several dozen publications targeted at a range of audiences (in some cases, several for each audience), and a full-time public relations department.

"Often [an outside consultant]— someone who is objective and can walk away from his or her recommendations— is in the best position to conduct an audit."

An audit was conducted by staff, under the direction of the board. A series of 50 formal interviews was conducted, along with a host of informal conversations. Among those interviewed were professional staff, medical staff, clerical and administrative staff, community leaders, selected trade media, and hospital volunteers.

The net result was the discovery of a major internal communications problem. Professional staff members were bitter that the public relations department had failed to arrange media interviews and garner the appropriate recognition for their contributions. Internal publications were not addressing such important audiences as the large blue-collar staff of orderlies, clerks, nurses' aides, and office workers. The trustees suspected there was a problem somewhere but didn't know how to address it. The public relations department, in turn, received minimal feedback from staff members about their activities. And, perhaps most damaging, the center was seen as uncaring by the community. In short, the internal communications process had broken down, relationships with the national and local media were hit-or-miss, and relationships with the community were deteriorating. Once identified, a plan to address these problems could be put in place.

2. A distinguished liberal arts college faced a unique opportunity. Preeminent in its field, the institution was approaching its centennial. It would be a chance to rally alumni and community supporters and to build for the future—a chance that only comes once in the life of any organization.

Yet despite an outstanding record of educational service and an impeccable reputation, the institution was not ready to take full advantage of the range of opportunities the centennial presented. Admired by alumni, students, and parents, the institution had kept a low profile, even within this closed circle.

An outside public relations firm was hired to conduct an audit to identify public relations opportunities arising from the centennial observance. Interviews were conducted with faculty, administrators, alumni, students, fundraising staff, and administrators of sister organizations. Ultimately, the interviews revealed weaknesses in the existing public relations staff and its practices. No comprehensive communications program existed. Opportunities to showcase distinguished faculty for alumni, the community, and in the media were missed or ignored. Major news stories emanating from the school were never told. Bright, promising students turned elsewhere for an education. Fundraising programs fell short of their potential.

What the audit did for the school was to identify the public relations areas where changes and an additional investment might pay off handsomely. It defined the basic questions the institution needed to address in order to plan a successful centennial.

As these examples suggest, an effective public relations audit leads naturally into planning for the future. Strengths disclosed by an audit should be sustained and any weaknesses should be corrected.

As previously mentioned, there are overlapping aspects to public relations planning: the targeting of specific audiences, the refinement of public relations objectives, the selection of particular strengths and techniques, and the formulation of a budget. A budget is one aspect that clearly quantifies a plan and helps management set priorities.

BUDGETING

Planners need a general sense of a budget's parameters before they can put detailed plans on paper. For instance, when planning a targeted public relations campaign, publicists should know beforehand how much the organization can spend on such a campaign.

For nonprofit groups, the total public relations budget will vary with the nature of the organization. Groups dedicated to affecting public opinion most likely will earmark a larger share of their overall budget to communications than will organizations that mainly provide services.

Establishing the parameters of a public relations budget can also spare an organization's staff and supporters a lot of disappointment: with clearly defined parameters in place, no one will expect a designer dress on a thrift-shop budget. An organization needn't spend a lot of money to have a public relations program, but the less money it has, the more effective its strategies must be.

A Sample Budget Format

In the final analysis, budgeting comes down to making choices—choices about how and where an organization wants to spend available monies. Can internal staff and volunteers handle the work, or is outside professional help needed? What new materials—brochures, audiovisual displays, and so on—are needed, or can the organization rely on existing

". . . when planning a targeted public relations campaign, publicists should know beforehand how much the organization can spend on such a campaign."

materials? How will changing organizational priorities affect public relations expenditures? Example 3 offers some guidelines.

EXAMPLE 3.	Budget Decisions
Budget Items	Choices Affecting Budgets
Staff	Organization's pay scale, previous professional experience, use of outside counsel, freelance help, volunteers
Staff training	In-house training, continuing education courses, conferences, seminars
Professional fees	Public relations counsel, marketing and advertising consultants, photographers, filmmakers, videotape and film editors, graphic designers, publicists, event coordinators, writers, fundraising consultants, direct-mail consultants, public-opinion researchers
Design and printing of materials	Special design elements (concept, layouts, pasteups); special artwork (illustration); typography; photography; quantity and type of material printed (newsletters, brochures, news releases, information kits, reports, invitations); paper quality; use of color; method of binding; special effects
Production of audiovisual materials	Studio rentals, engineer and technician fees, rental of cameras and recording equipment, mixing and editing fees, quantity of audiovisual release prints produced, special packaging, displays
Distribution of materials	Quantity and frequency of materials distribution, use of marketing firms, packaging, postage, shipping, list purchase or rental
Travel	Mileage reimbursement, bus/plane/train tickets, taxi fare, meals, lodging
Special events	Equipment rental and purchase, space rental, honoraria, advertising and/or marketing costs, catering, entertainment, signage, programs, name tags, flowers, photographers
Special production	Signage, displays, exhibits, posters, bumper stickers, buttons, billboards, registration fees
Out-of-pocket expenses	Photocopying, messenger, telephone, facsimile transmission, transcription, word processing

For Small Organizations: Budget Trimming

The budget process, by necessity, must allow for cutbacks and the hard choices required to fit a program to available but limited resources. Funding may not always be available for special projects and monies originally earmarked for certain programs ultimately may be needed for other projects.

On occasion, these economic "realities" may reflect poorly laid out organizational priorities. Too often, communications budgets are trimmed for the benefit of other programs simply because the importance of communications is not adequately understood. Many organizations do not even have a line in their budgets for communications or public relations, relying on program heads instead to "find room" in their budgets for necessary public relations activities throughout the year.

When the red flag of financial distress goes up, watch out for the quick initial reaction and recommendations to cut "extra" program money, leaving a staff intact but with no money to get jobs accomplished, or, alternatively, a staff reduced but with no commensurate reduction in program objectives. A careful balance must be found between this Scylla and Charybdis, as neither approach makes much sense.

Even in the smallest and tightest budgets, there should be room for reductions in public relations expenditures without compromising quality. Expensive projects such as videos and full-color brochures might have to be deferred until money is available. When push comes to shove, there are ways to bring down the costs of almost every item on your budget, especially production costs.

When the budget needs trimming, here are some places to look:

Design. Design and consulting fees vary enormously. Shop around. Students are available for special projects, often at reduced rates or on a volunteer basis. Don't forget existing volunteers as a possible source of such talent. To avoid overtime charges, charges for additional design costs once the project is underway, and extensive delays, make design and typesetting changes at the *earliest* stage possible.

Printing. Again, shop around. Obtain bids from several printing shops. There are a variety of factors that drive up the cost of printing, including the number of photos used, the quality of the paper stock, special design elements, the amount of ink coverage on a page, and the method of reproduction. Specific choices can dramatically affect the cost of printing. Consult a printer early in the project.

Distribution. Advance planning is the best way to reduce postage and shipping costs—the more time allowed, the less money spent. Become familiar with the different classes of postal rates currently available. Your local post office may be willing to help in planning and estimating the cost of a large mailing.

Photographers. Using a volunteer photographer can save you the substantial fees charged by professional photographers ($250 to $2,000 per

"Too often, communications budgets are trimmed for the benefit of other programs simply because the importance of communications is not adequately understood."

day). But bad work is always a bad bargain. Recruit students for small jobs, but ask to see examples of their work before you make a commitment. Photos also may be available for relatively small fees from commercial stock houses.

Video. Quality video work requires professional-level personnel and expensive production services. Everything else is home movies. Rather than undercut your message with an amateurish video, lower your sights. A high-quality slide show can be professionally produced at a fraction of the cost of a videotape of similar length.

Newsletters. Try to use copies of news releases and newspaper clippings as a way to replace internal newsletters and the like. (They're usually the source of "news" for internal newsletters anyway.) Unless an organization is a large one, employee benefits and other news from the personnel department—probably the most important aspect of employee communications—usually can be handled through internal memoranda.

Review the outside readership of newsletters. How many are "dead" names being carried even though no one remembers why? Is the complimentary list too large? Are there too many copies left over after each print run?

Desktop Publishing. Desktop publishing has revolutionized the way many organizations produce brochures, newsletters, annual reports, and other publications (see the next chapter). With a good software application, even small nonprofits are now able to turn out visually appealing, professional-looking materials on minuscule budgets, thereby eliminating expensive and time-consuming typesetting and design fees.

Pro Bono Public Relations Counsel. Major advertising and public relations agencies often provide *pro bono* counsel as a way of extending services to their communities (it's good public relations) and building additional links to groups with whom or for whom they might want to work someday. In fact, when an agency has minimal experience in a field in which it wants to develop a track record, it is often to its advantage to take on small groups on a *pro bono* basis.

Approach the principals of these agencies with letters soliciting their assistance. If they can't help, they might know who can. Ask them for the names of creative people who do outside freelance work; freelancers often produce good work at a substantially lower rate than that charged by most agencies. Either the agency or an independent freelancer might even be willing, for a small fee, to conduct an audit or fashion a public relations plan for you, regardless of whether there's funding available to keep them on retainer or to put their plan into effect.

"With a good software application, even small nonprofits are now able to turn out visually appealing . . . materials on minuscule budgets. . . ."

BRAINSTORMING

Many organizations have found that brainstorming is a useful way of identifying strategies to get their messages out. Successful brainstorming quickly produces a wealth of ideas while engaging a number of people in the formative stages of a public relations plan. To be successful, brainstorming sessions must be open and encourage participation. They should also be carefully focused on achieving relevant results.

To provide the necessary focus, appoint a leader for the sessions. The leader should quickly sketch in background information and present the problems to be solved. The participants—five to eight is ideal—should understand that the purpose is not to evaluate suggestions but rather to generate as many ideas as possible, even if they seem frivolous or unworkable. Participants should be discouraged from passing judgments that create an atmosphere of competitiveness or self-censorship, which only inhibits the flow of ideas. One person should be designated to take detailed notes.

A more critical evaluation of the suggestions should then be conducted in a separate session by a smaller group. This group will select some of the ideas with a view to creating a workable, financially feasible plan that delivers a consistent message. The plan must fit comfortably with the overall management objectives of the organization and have the approval and support of the executive director and board of directors (as appropriate). A timetable and budget should then be built into the plan, as should a schedule of regular evaluations designed to measure actual accomplishments to date against your original objectives.

"To be successful, brainstorming sessions must be open and encourage participation."

2 Developing Informational Materials

"The biggest communications medium in the world is the sky. Though some advertisers use banners towed by airplanes and skywriting, most communicators completely ignore this medium. The Goodyear blimp is perhaps the best known promotional use of the sky. If public relations people were to turn their creative vision toward the sky on occasion, many novel and newsworthy uses of the medium undoubtedly would be developed."

—Richard Weiner
Guide to Public Relations Services

Do you need to market a new program or service? Find new support for a cause? Raise additional funds? Mobilize more volunteers? Whatever your goals, you will need to create a range of materials that effectively delivers your messages.

The standard public relation tools used by nonprofit groups include brochures and pamphlets, newsletters, annual reports, and videos. Although these tools remain relevant to the work of most organizations today, in many instances they have been supplemented by new technologies ranging from computer disks to facsimile transmissions and electronic mail.

New reproduction and distribution technologies have also increased the production options available to groups that wish to create a brochure or distribute a newsletter. With the advent of desktop publishing software, we have all become graphic designers and newsletter publishers. Recent advances in color photocopying allow us to upgrade flyers, pamphlets, posters, and presentations. Today, a professional-looking presentation is only as far as the nearest photocopy and print shop.

New reproduction technologies are also faster and more flexible than traditional production and printing processes, allowing us to target our messages more carefully and to disseminate information more quickly. What may have taken weeks to produce 10 or 15 years ago can now be turned around overnight.

But every revolution has a downside. For many people, the explosion of information technologies has resulted in "communications overload," making it harder and harder for nonprofits to get their messages across. The challenge is to create media that will deliver your messages in ways that cut through the clutter.

CUTTING THROUGH THE CLUTTER

Brochures

Despite the increasing range of new media and new production technologies, many groups still elect to produce a brief organizational brochure first.

A descriptive piece that outlines a group's mission, activities, and programs can be used to build credibility. However much the task of writing and producing such a piece may appear to be straightforward, it's easier said than done. For a new organization, finding the language and images that best tell your story is both a difficult and important exercise. The finished product—the new brochure—should project the character and credibility of your group. For better or worse, it may also shape perceptions of your organization for years to come. As a result, creating an organizational brochure is much like looking at yourself in the mirror. You want to like what you see. Sometimes a lot of rearranging and fussing is needed before you are satisfied.

A brochure can describe the central mission of an organization or simply promote a project. It can be used to raise funds, to celebrate an anniversary, to promote a program or service, or to recruit volunteers. Yet to be effective, it should speak directly to the interests of one or more of your audiences. Before it can inform, motivate, or inspire, it must link their interests to the mission of the organization. An effective brochure

"A descriptive piece that outlines a group's mission, activities, and programs can be used to build credibility."

should actually talk about the reader. It should be market-driven. And it should be carefully conceived and prepared. The actual task of writing and producing such a piece can be daunting.

Before you attempt to write copy or fashion a design, ask yourself the following questions:

- What is the message we want to communicate?
- With whom do we want to communicate? Who are our key audiences? Who is the ideal reader of our brochure?
- What kind of response do we want from our readers? (i.e., what do we want people to think or do after reading our brochure? Join the organization? Ask questions? Send a check? Volunteer their services? Come to an event?)
- How should the brochure be written and designed to elicit the response we want? Does our message lend itself to extensive copy, photographs, graphs, or charts?

Once you've answered these questions you can begin the creative work that needs to be done to cut through the clutter and capture the attention of your audience.

Moving beyond the first brochure, the key to success in creating printed materials is to make sure that each subsequent piece is as necessary and focused as the first. To that end, thematic and design elements should be linked by the use of similar formats, matching or complementary colors, and compatible typefaces and layouts.

As a group becomes an organization and as an organization emerges as an institution, the pressure to create more and more printed material grows. As programs grow, organizations tend to produce brochures and printed pieces apace, responding to situations as they arise rather than creating new opportunities. And with each new piece, objectives can get fuzzy, design elements can get out of sync, and styles can become inconsistent. The result can be a hodgepodge of materials that eventually needs to be repackaged and a communications strategy that needs to be reinvented.

To maintain a consistent message and style in printed materials as your organization grows, some planning at the start will help. The more an organization is able to focus on its message and audiences at the outset, the more effective and professional its communications will be over the longer term.

As in every component of a public relations effort, it's a good idea to appoint a central decision-maker with responsibility for informational materials early on.

". . . the key to success in creating printed materials is to make sure that each subsequent piece is as necessary and focused as the first."

Newsletters and Membership Publications

Newsletters can be used to inform and motivate special audiences.

To be effective, a newsletter should have a clear sense of its readers and their links to the organization. Whether it offers chatty news and features about volunteers or employees, promotes the organization's work in order to garner additional support, or informs existing (and potential) members about organizational issues, a newsletter—and this is vital—should demonstrate an understanding of its readers and their interests.

The most successful newsletters are those that contain news and information readers can use—news, in other words, that is timely and informative. A good newsletter teaches. It is written in a style that enhances its readability, with headlines and subheads that capture the reader's attention. It should be written and designed to be read thoroughly. If you harbor the suspicion that no one bothers to read your newsletter, it's probably time to retool it.

The frequency of your newsletter should be determined by the pace at which your organization generates news and by the need of its readership to be kept informed. It should not deliver old news or stale information. Nevertheless, budget constraints often limit an organization's ability to produce and distribute a newsletter on a regular basis. Just remember, the longer the downtime between issues, the harder it is to recapture readers. Additionally, infrequent publication often translates into larger production budgets, which are needed to create a lasting impact.

Publications soliciting support or serving as membership premiums tend to be glossier than the average newsletter, with more in-depth editorial coverage and better graphics. These organizational magazines usually go beyond news to cover more broadly the stories, issues, and personalities "behind" the news. As the care and nurturing of donors is often high on the priority list of most nonprofits, the premium approach is one you may want to incorporate into your publications planning, but with one caveat: the development and regular publication of an organizational magazine requires considerable resources.

Below is a list of ideas concerning the development of publications.

Content and Format. Obviously, what you communicate in a publication will be dictated by your organization's objectives. News stories, columns, and regular features—and how they appear on the page—shape how the reader perceives your organization. Prose should be kept simple, clear, and concise. Good editorial design will make the publication more readable. Editorial features to consider for a newsletter include:

- news and feature stories about the organization
- Q&A sections

"... a newsletter ... should demonstrate an understanding of its readers and their interests."

- member, volunteer, or staff feedback
- person-on-the-street interviews
- poll and survey information
- news items about the industry or your organization's area of specialization
- publications and new products
- new resources
- employee/volunteer profiles
- employee/volunteer news
- statistical information
- reprints of major policy statements or speech excerpts
- reprints of media coverage (with permission)
- bylined columns
- letters to the editor
- calendar of events

For some organizations, an issue-oriented publication that provides perspectives on a single issue or a variety of related issues as well as updates on the organization's activities and positions may be appropriate.

Photography and Illustration. Quality photography can make a newsletter, adding interest and focusing a reader's attention on key items and stories. Illustrations and/or artwork can be used for the same purpose. Both will increase your budget, but the added impact can be invaluable and so the extra expense should be incorporated into your planning from the beginning. The "extras" might include photographers' fees, film-processing fees, the cost of screening photographs for printing purposes, and additional printing costs.

If you plan to use photographs of individuals in promotional literature, you will need releases from those individuals granting you permission to use their images.

Design and Layout. Most newsletters are formatted for an 11" x 17" sheet (cut from a 25" x 38" sheet) and folded in half for an 8½" x 11" page. This format can be expanded with additional sheets, yielding eight or more pages (in multiples of four). Sheet size can vary, of course, though oversized sheets will increase your costs. The type of paper can range from coated stock to newsprint, from a matte finish to a textured look, and from a heavier bond to lighter-weight stock. Sixty-pound paper stock is relatively common.

In terms of design, a newsletter should have a consistent look from one issue to the next. A design can allow for the use of different-sized but related elements (for flexibility), as long as it organizes the newsletter's graphic components and helps order the editorial content. A good design makes layout and typesetting decisions simpler, easier, and faster.

Annual Reports

Many states now require nonprofit institutions and foundations to file an annual report in order to keep their tax-exempt status. Similarly, audited financial reports are usually required by foundations or corporate givers considering funding requests. Although the primary aim of an annual report is to provide information on the financial condition of an organization, more often than not the report becomes an organizational showcase and a fundraising tool used to recognize and mobilize donors.

The annual reports produced by nonprofits are often similar to those produced in the for-profit world. Each year, publicly held companies report to stakeholders—shareholders, employees, staff, the investment community, and, of course, the Securities and Exchange Commission, which requires regular statements—on their operations and financial condition. It has become standard operating procedure among corporate communications departments to create profusely illustrated, handsomely composed reports that can cost $5 a copy or more to produce (with print runs in the hundreds of thousands), not including staff and freelance time.

"An effective annual report can rally various stakeholders, building the case for continued support."

For nonprofits, an annual report serves an additional function as a promotional document, providing a forum in which an organization's mission and achievements can be outlined and a vision of its future can be mapped out. An effective annual report can rally various stakeholders, building the case for continued support. And, since it often provides the broadest reach of any internally produced publication, it may be the single most important piece an organization develops during the course of a year. For all these reasons, an annual report is usually worth the extra effort, time, and expense required to produce it.

An annual report generally takes from three to nine months to write, design, and produce. Much depends on how elaborate the report will be (number of photos and/or artwork used), the type and amount of copy required (is a special essay going to be commissioned?), and the internal clearance procedure. Is one person or department responsible for creating it, or will it be developed by committee? How many people have editorial input? How many will need to see the design? What kind of design/production team will tackle the report? Do photos need to be taken or will stock pictures do?

Some preliminary planning is always helpful. A meeting with the organization's senior executive and/or senior staff should be arranged to discuss the report's purpose, its possible themes and design, its utility over the course of the coming year, and when it should appear. A budget for producing the report should also be discussed and agreed on.

Authority for developing and producing the report should be delegated. If at all possible, the report should be made the responsibility of one staff member or department; the writing, editing, and design should be supervised by one person. In most cases, financial and audited information will be supplied by the organization's comptroller or accountant.

Questions of Format and Style. Even though most nonprofits do not have the budget to produce an elaborate annual report, your document can be just as persuasive and professional-looking as any corporate piece. Typically, a nonprofit annual report includes the following elements:

1. A message or letter from the organization's leadership framing the group's achievements and goals. This message might describe the challenges of the past year, identify future prospects, outline the needs of the organization, and show how they were or can be fulfilled.

   The message usually comes in the form of a letter from the chair of the board, the president, and/or the executive director. The copy should be kept simple and should highlight overarching themes, special programs, and new activities. If you think of the entire report as a single story, this introductory message would be the lead, summarizing the who, what, when, where, why, and how of the organization.

2. A list of the members of the board of trustees and officers of the organization.

3. A financial statement or a balance sheet of assets and liabilities and an income and expense breakdown. Usually the financial statement covers the past tax or fiscal year. For most nonprofits, it's helpful to include some information on donations and how they impact both revenues and expenses, at least in broad terms. Public charities are often criticized for the amount of money they spend on management, fundraising, overhead, and public relations versus the amount they allocate for actual programs and services. Financial information over and above the audit can address these issues.

4. Highlights of the past year's programmatic efforts and directions. Information can be handled program-by-program, by organizational structure, even by audience. The

structure of your report will depend on how your programs can best be explained, as well as on the politics of your organization. The point to remember is that your message should dictate the structure. Structure should not dictate content.

5. A brief history of the organization.

6. A list of major donors. A donor roster can be used to frame an appeal for additional help and solicit future contributions by saluting past donors. It can even become part of an overall discussion of how the group functions.

These are the elements found in most annual reports, though many groups choose to take their report a step further, producing a showpiece that, with a little luck, generates new interest in the organization, enthusiasm for its programs, and funding for the future.

There are several ways to inject interest and a sense of style into an annual report. Consider, for example, using the report to frame an extended article, perhaps written by a well-known journalist, on some major concern of your group. A photo essay might be in order. Original art can be used to add color and flavor. Or you might use a combination of pictures and words to profile a single event or honor a respected individual.

Obviously, the cover should attract the most attention. While it need not be gimmicky, overly extravagant, or even use four-color printing, it should have a strong design and be appropriate to the organization's mission. An arts group needs one kind of statement, a research organization another, and an educational group still another.

Posters

Posters are a form of advertisement and are often framed as mementos. They can be part of an advertising or promotional campaign, or produced specifically for a special event or to celebrate an anniversary.

As mentioned earlier, you can incorporate advertising art or artwork from an annual report (the cover, for example) into a poster design. If you already have a color separation or other camera-ready art that simply requires type, you can save an enormous production expense by adapting it to create a poster.

Other Ways to Spread the Word

T-shirts replaced buttons and bumper stickers some time ago as the preferred way to spread the word. More recently, tote bags have been transformed into walking advertisements by art museums, public libraries, performing arts groups, and public television stations. The totes have quickly been followed by other merchandise—umbrellas, clocks, paperweights, notepads, tapes, CDs, limited-edition prints, and so on. Many of these items are used to spur membership or are presented as giveaways at benefits. There are novelty companies in most areas that can produce a range of items with an organization's logo, name, and/or a short message.

Bumper stickers and buttons sporting all kinds of clever slogans were popular in the 1970s. In some areas, they appear to be making a comeback. (More recently, pins and ribbons have become popular.) Buttons, in particular, are useful at public events and rallies. They are also cheap (depending on design), quickly produced, and portable. But before you order a few thousand, think seriously about who would wear one, and for how long.

AUDIO/VISUALS

Slide Shows

The use of audiovisual presentations has become increasingly common among nonprofits. Quite often, speeches, news conferences, annual meetings, and planning sessions are enhanced by visual materials that illustrate and supplement the written or spoken word.

Slide-presentation formats range from front-screen-projected, manually advanced, one-projector shows to multiprojector slide/sound presentations utilizing computer-controlled programming, professional narration, and musical soundtracks.

As with any printed piece, the planning for a slide presentation should start with an examination of your objectives and audiences. You should also determine how the presentation will be used—that is, whether it will stand on its own or illustrate a prepared talk or presentation.

Your presentation should be developed with the help of a *storyboard*—the method used by ad agencies to develop TV commercials. A board measuring 27" x 27" will hold about forty 3" x 5" index cards, enough to work up a four- to five-minute slide presentation. Each card should represent a single slide frame. On the left side of each card, sketch out or insert the desired illustration. On the right, add the narration. If there is to be music or other production effects, note these to the right of the narration. The story unfolds as cards are placed on the board. Continuity can be strengthened by shifting cards or adding transitions.

Producing the Slide Show. Once the presentation has taken shape as a storyboard, it's time to think about photography, artwork, and, budget permitting, a soundtrack. The photography component of a presentation is obvious. Either the photos will be shot in-house, or the services of a professional photographer will be required. Artwork may be needed as illustrations or to create titles—that is, names, lists, quotes— that are superimposed on images or are used as stand-alone slides. You can use printed typeset copy, rub-on transfer letters, or computer-generated type to create titles or graphs, reshooting the slide against a colored paper background. If your budget permits, a commercial slide house can handle it all for you.

If you decide to create the title slides in-house, you'll need a camera lens with close-up capabilities, a copy stand, and some kind of camera stand. (A tripod is best.) Retain plenty of white space around the letters. Remember, most of what the audience sees will be projected on a 6' x 6' screen positioned up to 70 feet away. Can you read your slides without magnification at a distance of 12 inches? If the answer is yes, they'll probably be legible.

Scriptwriting is an art all its own. Your messages and style should be simple and direct. Avoid using subordinate clauses. Keep the voice active rather than passive. And be sure the words match the images on the screen.

"Scriptwriting is an art all its own. Your messages and style should be simple and direct."

Overhead Presentations

Overhead presentations are an inexpensive alternative to slides when a stand-alone presentation isn't needed. Acetate overheads can project images and color as well as copy. Although the images will be neither as bright nor as colorful as those produced by slides, the technology can be used without having to dim the lights—an obvious plus for any presentation that is built around give-and-take between a speaker and his or her audience.

A Word About Videos

High-quality video creates an impact far greater than print or slides. It can also be expensive, so before moving ahead:

- have an audience in mind for the final product
- be sure you're committed to the medium as the most effective way to reach the audience you have in mind
- use professional help

The public is accustomed to high production values. To be effective, your video will have to match those values. You'll need a solid script, on-screen "talent," a production crew that includes a camera operator and sound technician, an editor, and an editing studio.

A video is produced in three stages: script development and talent recruitment; the actual shooting of the video; and the post-production work, which includes editing and sound mixing. The most expensive items in video production are the camera, the lighting and sound crews, and the editing. Crews are usually hired on a per-diem basis, so their time must be used efficiently to keep costs down. Videos that require shoots in a variety of locations are usually more costly to produce than those shot in a single location. Editing talent and studio space is hired by the hour or by the day. Again, time is of the essence.

Computerized graphics and animation can also be expensive. If money is a consideration, these techniques should be avoided in favor of edited live action, quality sound, and music.

When all is said and done, a good script is the key to a good video. It is also the key to an efficient production. Scripts should include both an audio and a visual component, usually written as two columns on a page, audio on the left, visuals on the right. Again, make sure the audio reflects the visuals, and vice versa.

Getting Started. The audio component is often written first to assure that your key messages will be incorporated into the final product. The visual component is then developed with an eye to providing images that not only track the audio but enhance it. Individuals who will appear in the video as spokespeople or the subjects of interviews need to be found. Locations must be scouted. A final script will emerge once these and similar decisions are made. Production should only be scheduled once a final script is approved.

An experienced video producer and/or scriptwriter can be of enormous help. He or she will work with you to avoid script choices that run up costs (e.g., using multiple locations when one will do). An experienced producer can also accelerate the script-development process by securing the necessary crew and making arrangements for the editing.

In similar fashion, a tight script will make the production crew's job easier. With such a script in hand, they will have fewer spur-of-the-moment decisions to make and thus fewer opportunities to err. A high-

" . . . a good script is the key to a good video."

quality tape will, in turn, make the editor's job easier. In a real sense, the medium is built one layer at a time.

FINDING TALENT

Hiring a Graphic Designer

Graphic designers can help translate your organization's mission and message into something visually appealing. The work of a good designer will also help you create promotional material with the kind of punch and impact that cuts through the information clutter.

To find graphic designer candidates for an assignment, first ask for referrals from your board members, staff, and friends. Design firms are listed in the Yellow Pages. Professional associations also make referrals.

Collect résumés and portfolios, review them, and set up an interview with a designer whose work you like. Then ask yourself and the designer-candidate the following questions:

- What do you like about the designer's work? What don't you like?
- What kinds of assignments has s/he handled?
- How did s/he approach these assignments?
- What size budgets has s/he worked with?
- Will the designer arrange and supervise the printing of the piece?
- How well has s/he worked with other clients?
- Is s/he someone you can work with?
- How will the job be billed? By the hour? By the job?

Once you have narrowed the field, obtain estimates (including expenses) from the remaining candidates. And be sure to check references before you make a final decision.

"The designer will be an integral part of the group working on the project. . . ."

The designer will be an integral part of the group working on the project, be it a volunteer committee or a group of staff members. That means the designer has to be kept informed and perhaps even invited to project planning meetings. To do a proper job, he or she will need to know the message you want to communicate, the audience for that message, the focus of the piece, its length, and whether photos or other visuals will be used. The designer will also need to know your budget for design and production. Last but not least, a timetable will have to be established.

Ask the designer to read copy for the piece. (Don't assume a designer will do this automatically.) Ask for several design ideas, and when these are presented, speak your mind when you like—or don't like—what you see. Be specific in your comments, provide direction when you think it will lead to a better result, and expect some give-and-take before a design that works emerges.

The designer will produce a *mock-up, comp,* or *dummy* to give you a sense of what the finished piece will look like. It should show how the type and photos will be positioned, how headlines will look in relation to the copy, and how the brochure will "communicate" your message. After you have made changes and/or corrections and a final version has been approved, the designer will prepare a *mechanical* for the printer.

Finding a Writer

Writing talent is critical to the success of any communications effort. And yet, although most nonprofits have neither staff nor volunteers whose only responsibility is writing, it is a function that is usually managed in-house. As a result, program directors find themselves writing brochures; executive directors write the annual report.

On occasion, a writer from outside the organization may be needed to draft a technical piece, write a particularly important speech, or craft a script. Or you may simply want to weed out some of the jargon that inevitably creeps into copy produced internally. A professional writer can help. For technical material, you'll want to find a writer familiar with the subject matter. Speechwriting, scriptwriting, and direct-mail writing require someone with experience. Newsletter writing may call for a journalist.

Finding professional writers is not always easy. Try to get referrals from colleagues in organizations similar to your own, from your contacts in the media, and from associations of public relations and communications executives. Writing samples should be collected and interviews arranged. Read through the samples and identify what you like and what you don't like. Ask the candidate why assignments were handled the way they were. Decide whether he or she is a person with whom you'd like to work.

Before you hire, have a thorough discussion of fee arrangements—by the project or by the hour—and determine how rewrites will be handled.

Hiring and Working with a Printer

Solicit bids from at least three printers. (Your designer should be able to provide names, and other nonprofits are also a resource.)

> *"On occasion, a writer from outside the organization may be needed to draft a technical piece, write a particularly important speech, or craft a script."*

"A good
printer will
explain the
available
options and
help you think
through your
decisions."

In order to provide a bid, a printer will need certain information about the job to be done, including quantity, trim size, page count, special type needs and color requirements, the paper stock, and your due date. Once a printer submits a bid, review the minimum charges and samples of work done by that shop. Check references, and double-check to make sure the printer has the equipment required to do the job and can do the work needed (rather than farm it out to subcontractors).

Instead of simply acceptng the lowest bid, find a printer who will be easy to work with. It will make a difference. A good printer will explain the available options and help you think through your decisions. (A good graphic designer can provide similar assistance.) Talk to the printer about budget constraints and how you might achieve the effects you need at lower cost. Finally, get a written estimate and a guaranteed delivery date before you release the job.

Finding a Video Producer

To find a video producer, start with the Yellow Pages. Then check with local public-access studios and the film departments of local colleges and universities. You can also ask people at organizations like your own about the independent producers or video-production companies they use.

Feel free to ask prospective producers or production companies to provide a tape with examples of their best work. If they won't, don't consider them. A producer is not someone you should hire "cold."

Feel free as well to ask a producer about his or her work. Most video producers are familiar with the technical aspects of their profession and will be able to answer any questions you're likely to come up with. By asking questions, you'll also be giving the producer an idea of the complexity of your project—something he or she will want to consider before agreeing to work with you. You may even be able to solicit free advice on conceptualizing the various aspects of your project.

It can also be advantageous to view a producer's demo tape at his or her offices, which gives you a chance to see the staff and how they seem to handle other jobs. Choosing a video producer is only the first step. You'll have to work with this person, and so you should have a sense of how effectively this person works before you make your decision.

Remember, price is not necessarily the most important factor. Often, the difference between the least and most expensive video producer or production company will be minimal.

WRITING COPY YOURSELF

When it comes to writing, there is a deceptively simple formula to follow. It's called KISS, short for "Keep It Simple (Stupid)." This doesn't mean you should "dumb down" complex, sophisticated material. Rather, it is a call to write with the kind of clarity that enhances communication and understanding—even when the material is complex.

Several years ago *The Wall Street Journal* ran a piece about computing a writer's "fog index"—that is, an index that measures just how convoluted, wordy, or unclear writing can be. The formula for identifying "gaseous" writing, according to the Gunning Mueller Clear Writing Institute, is as follows:

1. Find the average number of words per sentence in a writing sample 100 to 200 words long. Treat independent clauses, even in the same sentence, as separate sentences.

2. Calculate the percentage of words having three or more syllables. Don't count capitalized words or verbs that become three syllables by adding *es* or *ed*.

3. Add the average sentence length to the percentage of big (three or more syllables) words. Then multiply the total by .04. The resulting number is the years of schooling needed to understand what you're reading.

The moral of the story? Professional writers write simply. *The Catcher in the Rye* has a fog index of six, as does most of the material in *TV Guide*. *The Wall Street Journal, Time,* and *Newsweek* each average about 11.

Writing Style

There is only one writing style for you, one that is singularly yours. Whether you're writing a commencement speech, an annual report, a news release about the appointment of an executive director, or a feature story on some good work your organization recently accomplished, your style—the process by which you approach the task, your universe of words, and your ability to express yourself—remains distinctively yours. The trick is to adapt it to fit the occasion.

Brochure writing requires one approach—reader-friendly prose that aims for clarity. Feature stories and personality profiles require another, and news stories require yet another. (The lead in a news story should include the most important facts within the first 30 words or so. Speech-

"The moral of the story? Professional writers write simply."

writing, which requires an approach all its own, is discussed at greater length below.)

The following tips, culled from a number of sources and our own experiences, should give you some ideas about how to manage and adapt your writing style to the project at hand.

Preparing to Write

It's not easy to begin writing. In fact, getting started is probably the hardest aspect of writing. If there were a book on how to overcome "writer's block," which often takes the form of procrastination—doing anything else but writing—it would be a sure best-seller. But while there is no one cure, there are several ways to deal with the symptoms.

Create an outline. Start by outlining your ideas on paper. It will help you organize your thoughts and provide a structure for your creativity.

Look "down the tunnel." Before you start, figure out where you want to finish. Imagine yourself about to enter a tunnel and picture an image at the end of it.

Procrastinate. Give in to the feeling, but give in creatively—doodle, concentrate on something else, go to sleep but get up in the middle of the night and try again. The human brain is an extremely logical, methodical, and orderly center for the organization and digestion of information. By focusing on other things, you let your subconscious do most of the work. Even if you are not consciously concentrating on the task at hand, your mind will continue to consider it. So take your mind off the immediate writing task—but do so only after you've reviewed the materials once or twice and given thought to what you'd like the piece to do. Give it time and keep coming back to the task at hand, rejecting your openings until you come up with one you like. It may not be the one you end up with, but it's a start.

Use "mapping." Marilyn Hanf Buckley, a Berkeley professor, first came up with this idea, which is closer to doodling than outlining. Start by jotting down the story assignment in a circle in the center of a sheet of paper. Then draw lines, or "highways," radiating out from the circled assignment. Each "highway" should represent a train of thought. Next, relate facts, or "driveways," to a "highway," laying them out in sequence until you've exhausted that train of thought. You can even create "back roads"—wandering dotted lines that connect different "highways" and "driveways."

Below is example of mapping from *Editor & Publisher* about a story on the closing of a piano factory.

Write the way you speak. Well, almost the way you speak. According to Ethel Grodzins Romm's "Writing Guide" in *Editor & Publisher,* unedited writing is filled with repetition because we write the way we think. Speakers double back and double up to help their listeners, simply because the spoken word goes through the ear fast and only once. Linguists tell us that 50 percent of spoken English is redundant, filled with phrases such as "future plans," "past history," "mental telepathy," "typical example," and so on.

So write in a conversational style. Writing "conversationally" will steer your language clear of passive phrases, jargon, wordiness, and overblown sentences, all of which are common in professional writing. You don't talk like that, so why write like that?

Careful editing should eliminate the redundancies, the use of the passive voice, and convoluted syntax. Remember, it's always better to write something and then rewrite it than never to have written it at all.

Use words that count. Peter Jacobi, a writing consultant, tells his clients: "Consider the first five to ten words and make them count.

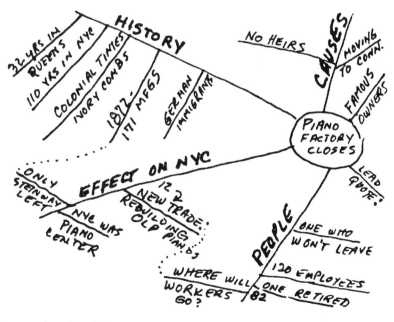

Source: *Editor & Publisher,* November 6, 1982. Reprinted with permission.

Consider the first sentence and make it count. Consider the first paragraph and make it count. Consider the lead so that it counts."

Use "peopling." Almost every story can be told from an individual's point of view. Show how people are affected. Describe who is doing the work, what their plans and visions are, what their experience is. Let people speak for themselves. Use dialogue, including quotes and actual bits of conversation. Use third-person narration (i.e., he said this or she did that) for straightforward appeals; use first-person narration if the piece is anecdotal, if it's a speech, or if there is humor involved.

State the facts. As John Ciardi, a magazine writer, once noted: "Never send an adjective on a noun's errand." Public relations professionals have to be careful about editorializing in news releases and most other materials. Except for a little hyperbole in editorials or "Letters to the Editor," take care to maintain your credibility when communicating with the media. Using charged adjectives and superlatives tends to make editors skeptical and diminishes your credibility. Let the readers draw their own conclusions based on the information presented. Of course, a skilled writer can help shape perceptions by the way he or she frames the information. In other words, if you think your project is exciting, don't say it's exciting; describe the program in a way that excites.

Attribute. Attribution is never having to say you are sorry. If someone else said it, be sure to give him or her credit. So many hoaxes have been perpetrated in journalism (leading, in one instance, to an ill-gotten Pulitzer Prize) that it's difficult to overplay the need to attribute. If you send a story to an editor, you have entered the world of journalism. Play by its rules. You'll never have to say you're sorry—to the editor, to your own organization, or to yourself.

Use "image" words. Follow the advice of Edward T. Thompson, former editor-in-chief of *Reader's Digest,* and use *first-degree words.* These are words that immediately bring an image to mind (*face* is a first-degree word). A second- or third-degree word has to bring a first-degree word to mind before it can be imagined (*visage* is a second-degree word, *countenance* a third-degree word).

Be brief. Use short words. Throw *unique* out the window and watch out for other superlatives as well. Keep your sentences short, your paragraphs short, and your stories only as long as they need to be.

Keep a fresh eye on your subject. Writing is an expression of the creativity in each of us; it should not be automatic.

". . . if you think your project is exciting, don't say it's exciting; describe the program in a way that excites."

Some final tips. Ethel Romm suggests that you observe the following simple rules before you give your work to someone else for a second opinion:

- Get rid of nearly every *it, this, that, who*, and *which*.

- Read your piece aloud, paying attention to the copy's rhythm. Take the naturalness of your normal conversation and put it into the piece.

- Make sure passive phrases need to be passive. Can you activate them?

- Don't "peter out" at the end of your piece. When you're done, end it. Usually you can lop off your closing remarks without sacrificing the effectiveness of your ending. There are only so many times you can say goodbye before your readers/editors will say the same to you.

Finally, write about things that interest you. If the subject matter doesn't interest you, and you don't write about it in an interesting fashion, it certainly won't interest your audience.

Editing and Copy Editing

There are about 650,000 words in the English language. Don't try to use them all in every news release you write. Instead, try to be your own best editor. The rules of the trade hold that good self-editors can cut 10 words for every 250 words they write.

To ensure consistency across a range of written materials, every organization should have a stylebook in which word usage, hyphenation, spelling, capitalization, and other style issues are addressed. If your organization's style is to use "Ms." instead of "Miss," be sure to use it consistently. If your organization's style calls for *theater* to be spelled with with an *er* instead of an *re*, it should appear that way in every piece of copy you produce. If for some reason you can't create a stylebook yourself, adopt one. Among those favored by professional copy editors are *The Chicago Manual of Style, Words Into Type, The New York Times' Manual of Style Usage*, and the *Associated Press Stylebook*.

Before your copy goes to the printer, someone acting as an editor *must* review it for credibility, accuracy, consistency, style, readability, and effectiveness.

In most nonprofits, professional staff handling public relations will also edit much of the material the organization creates for outside distribution. When you edit, put yourself in the writer's shoes and then put

"To ensure consistency across a range of written materials, every organization should have a stylebook. . . ."

yourself in those of the reader. First, read the entire piece through once without marking a thing. Now consider: What if a member of your target audience received and read that copy? Would it do what it is supposed to do? Would it make them angry? Would it bore them?

Next, go back and mark obvious misspellings and typographical errors. Then look at the opening and closing paragraphs—the parts to which readers pay so much attention. Are they interesting and effective? Remember, the second paragraph often makes for a better lead and the penultimate paragraph a better close, simply because it takes some writers time to work up a head of steam or shut down the engine.

Third, look at each word, then each sentence, then each paragraph. Watch for faulty grammar, convoluted syntax, the passive versus the active voice, clichés, unclear language, inconsequential quotes, redundancy, adjectives used instead of nouns, and overeditorializing.

Fourth, make sure the story *tracks:* the storyline should follow a logical sequence, both temporally (in the order the events occurred) and structurally (the piece should have some dramatic flow from paragraph to paragraph).

Fifth, check for accuracy. If you're not certain about a fact, ask the writer to back it up. The writer should of course recheck all facts and numbers. It is easy for a number to be wrong and for the editor not to notice. It's up to the writer to get it right.

Finally, make certain the headline and content match.

Proofreading

Eventually, everyone has to proofread copy, galleys, or page proofs against the original manuscript. Proofreading is a discipline. It demands concentration. Here are some hints:

- If it's a short piece, read it from beginning to end first. That way, you won't get so caught up in the language that you'll miss typographical and other mechanical errors.

- Be particularly careful about numbers and word breaks at the end of lines.

- Give yourself time to do a careful job. The earlier in the production process you catch an error, the less expensive it will be to fix. When correcting proofs from the typesetter or your own desktop operation, remember that mistakes will cost five to ten times more to correct in the next stage of production. It's cheaper to correct in galleys than in page proofs, cheaper in page proofs than in bluelines, and so on. One rule of thumb when

"The earlier in the production process you catch an error, the less expensive it will be to fix."

PROOFREADERS' MARKS AND SAMPLE COPY

⌞3	Delete	*tr*	Transpose		∀	Superscript
⌒	Close up	*eq. # or* ∨∧	Equalize space		⌃	Subscript
3	Delete and close up	⊏	Indent 1 em		?/	Question mark
↵	Push down lead that prints	*ld*	Insert lead between lines		!/	Exclamation point
ⓧ	Broken letter	*ld*	Take out lead		=/	Hyphen
#	Space or more space	*stet*	Let it stand		(/)	Parentheses
9	Reverse; turn over	ⓢ	Spell out		[/]	Brackets
¶	Begin a paragraph	⊢M⊣	Em dash		⌒ *or lig*	Use ligature
⊐⊏	Center	⊢N⊣	En dash		*wf*	Wrong font
]	Move to right	⊙	Period		*lf*	Lightface type
[	Move to left	⌃	Comma		*bf*	Boldface type
⌞⌟	Lower letters or words	;/	Semicolon		*rom*	Roman type
⌐⌐	Raise letters or words	:/	Colon		*ital*	Italic type
‖	Align type vertically	∀	Apostrophe or 'single quote'		*caps*	CAPITALS
―	Straighten line	∀/∀	Quotation marks		*sm. c.*	SMALL CAPITALS
∧	Insert from margin	*run on*	No paragraph		*lc*	Lower case

The following passage shows the use of proofreaders' marks. They are placed in the margins and corresponding marks are inserted within the copy to indicate where a change is to be made. If a line has more than one correction or change, the marginal proofreaders' marks are separated by diagonal lines.

For whatever reasons—and they are not entirely clear—dictionaries have become a sort of specialty of the English-speaking world. A possible explanation may be sought in the size of the vocabulary, since English seems to have more words and more uses for words—many more than 2 million named uses—than any other known language. Speakers of English have uncommon need for dictionaries, and Americans, who constitute the largest single body of English speakers and who have been uncommonly well provided with the means of buying reference works, have augmented this need with what would seem to be a mania for linguistic correctness, a zeal for rectitude which they have built into their elaborate school system. This, for whatever reason, the speakers of no other known language have ever brought to fruition such a work as the *Oxford English Dictionary* (also called *A New English Dictionary on Historical Principles*) whose editors endeavored to trace every use of every word that has ever gained wide currency in the native tongue. The creation of the modern American desk dictionary is scarcely less remarkable. American lexicography has its own glories and its own character. The founder of the American school was Noah Webster, whose *An American Dictionary of the English Language* (1828 and frequently revised and enlarged) was a truly remarkable work, especially for its day and place, a New world still very much a colony, socially and intellectually, of the old. Webster was an untiring and self-assertive as Samuel Johnson himself, and if he was less well read and probably less intellectually endowed, he suffered from no false modesty and he possessed a genius for definition. His work was rivaled in many ways by that of his onetime employee, Joseph E. Worcester, and the "War of the Dictionaries" waged between the successors to Websters volume and Worcester's *A Dictionary of the English Language* (1860), lent to lexicography the zest of a sporting event.

Source: *Webster's New World Dictionary, 2nd College Edition.* © 1980 by Simon and Schuster, a division of Gulf and Western Publishing.

considering a change: If it's essential, do it; if not, think about it first.

See the previous page for a list of commonly used proofreaders' marks. In proofing, indicate all corrections twice—once at the place the error occurs and then again opposite it in the margin.

THE PRINT PRODUCTION PROCESS

To ensure that the production of a printed piece proceeds relatively smoothly and on schedule, your staff and/or volunteers, graphic designer, and printer need to reach an understanding on clearing and approving the design, copy, and proofs.

A timetable, created with the designer and printer, can help guide you through the process by indicating who is responsible for the copy, design, and proofing at each stage of the job. Organizations that use desktop software will be able to condense the process, although decisions about copy, type, design, and art will be the same.

Step One—Copywriting

When submitting copy to a designer, typesetter, or printer, be sure to use standard 8½" x 11" white paper. (If the copy is on a diskette, be sure it's in a standard ASCII format.) Double-space the copy, leaving wide margins on the sides, top, and bottom. Try not to break a paragraph between pages. Number the pages consecutively and proof carefully.

Even at this early stage, decisions about the appropriate typeface, or *font,* for the main body of your copy will have to be made. There are four basic font styles: Roman, Text, Gothic, and Script. Type sizes are measured in points (a point equals approximately $1/72$ of an inch). Text copy usually runs 8 to 12 points. Consult a designer or typesetter to determine the best typeface for your job. (A hint: It's best to limit the use of different typefaces and sizes. Too much variety will confuse the reader's eye and deflect attention away from the message you're trying to convey.)

Copy should follow a rough layout, or dummy, that indicates where various design and graphic elements will appear. Desktop publishing software will guide you through this layout process.

For those using outside type and design services, the first step in the layout/composition process is to have your copy typeset as galleys.

"It's best to limit the use of different typefaces and sizes."

Step Two—The Galley

An outside typesetter will return your copy as long sheets called galleys. Ask for three sets—one for the proofreader and two for the designer. Proofread the galleys carefully against the original manuscript. Note any mistakes you may have made as well as those made by the typesetter. (Most typesetters won't charge you to correct mistakes they have introduced into your copy. Proofreaders usually note a typesetter's mistake with a circled "PE"—for "printer's error"—next to the appropriate proofreading mark. However, you will be charged for all "AAs"—"author's alterations.") Mark the galleys using standard proofreaders' marks (see page 41). Mark mechanical errors—type that is blurry or smudged, too light or too dark, or broken—as well. Don't expect your designer to proofread galleys; the copy is your responsibility.

Step Three—Dummy/Layout/Pasteup

The following terms are helpful to know for this phase of the production process.

The *layout,* or positioning of copy and graphics on a page, is usually determined at the start of a job. (Those using desktop publishing software will be able to develop and manipulate a layout on their computer.) A *dummy,* or *mock-up,* is constructed to show what the piece will look like. A *comp* is the camera-ready version of the piece as it will appear in print. *Pasteup,* the actual pasting up of copy and graphic elements, occurs several times during the process, including at the layout stage and later at the mechanical stage, when camera-ready art is being prepared for the printer. When designing printed material, a rough layout becomes a mock-up, which in turn forms the basis for a comp.

When examining a layout or mock-up, note how the paper is to be folded and how the copy and photos look next to one another. Decisions about the use of visual material and graphic elements, including how best to use different typefaces, photos, columns, and line art, should be made at this stage.

Line art includes rules, borders, cartoons, and pen-and-ink illustrations. It can be original artwork, or it can be purchased at art-supply stores, from your typesetter, or from your printer. (Desktop publishing software comes with its own art and graphics capabilities.) Line art does not need to be screened in order to be reproduced.

With help from your designer or printer, you should select a paper stock. Paper comes in different weights (e.g., 50-pound, 60-pound, or

"When designing printed material, a rough layout becomes a mock-up, which in turn forms the basis for a comp."

70-pound) and finishes (e.g., coated, uncoated, or textured). Factors to take into account when choosing a paper stock include your target audience, the quantity you plan to print, and your budget.

In the comp stage you can decide whether you want to print your piece in one, two, or four colors.

Step Four—Photographs

If photographs are to be used in the piece, they will need to be cropped and sized to fit the layout, then sent to a photo house for processing into a form that can be used by a printer to create an image on paper. Black-and-white photos are screened into *halftones,* a matrix (usually impressed on metal) of tiny dots that can be inked and reproduced; the more dots in the matrix, or *screen,* the better the reproduction will be. Black-and-white photos can also be given some depth and drama by using a second color to create a *duotone.* Black-and-white photos reproduced using a four-color process will have even more detail and texture.

Color photos need to be *separated* before they can be printed. The separation process actually begins with the original photo being rephotographed using filters which correspond to one of the primary colors—yellow, red, or blue—plus a fourth color, black. These four colors are then combined in varying proportions to produce the other colors of the spectrum. A reproduced color photo is usually composed of tiny, different-sized and -colored dots, some overlaying others, most adjacent to each other. The effect is full color.

Step Five—The Mechanical

The creation of *mechanicals* is the last step in the production process before the job goes to the printer. Once the copy and line art have been corrected and finalized, the designer or pasteup person takes the camera-ready material and pastes it up on sheets of special coated cardboard called *boards*; precisely sized blank spaces in the proper position are created for the photographs.

Step Six—Bluelines

Bluelines, which are supplied by the printer, are final page proofs with art and photographs included. They are exact images of the negatives that the printer has created from the mechanicals, and they are produced on special coated sheets of blue paper—thus the name bluelines, or *blues.*

Step Seven—Printing

The bluelines are returned to the printer with any corrections or comments written directly on the page. Watch for broken or obliterated type, photos that are too dark or too light, crooked rules, pictures without captions, and other irregularities. If you decide to make editorial revisions at this stage, you'll have to supply the printer with new camera-ready copy for the pages you have changed.

The last stage of proof involves F&Gs (shorthand for "folded and gathered sheets"), also known as *press sheets*, which allow you to examine the piece, in color or black-and-white, as it will appear in publication. If you are using color in the piece, check to make sure the colors are accurate and the registration is in sync. Although it is still possible to make changes at this late stage, the cost of doing so almost always rules against it.

3   Publicity

"In a free society, the independent communications medium is closer to having absolute sovereignty than any other element."
—Philip Lesley
Lesley's Public Relations Handbook

Media exposure is the single most important tool used by public relations practitioners to gain visibility for an organization, its issues, and/or its services.

Publicity is coverage in the media, be it print or electronic. As such, it can range from news stories, feature articles, and editorials in national or local newspapers, magazines, or trade journals to appearances on talk shows and news programs.

Publicists use a variety of informational materials (e.g., news releases and photos), vehicles (e.g., the telephone, faxes, mail), and settings (e.g., news conferences and special events) to get the attention of the media.

Not every contact with the media needs to result in a story, however. Becoming a trusted source of expert information can be invaluable for nonprofits. If you can help an editor develop a story idea—even if your organization isn't featured in that story—you will be on your way to establishing a useful long-term relationship. And that can work to your organization's advantage in any number of ways.

This chapter will examine how best to work with the media to promote your organization and publicize specific events. It includes information on how to:

- develop a publicity plan
- develop and use a media list
- create the materials needed to interest the media in a story
- generate coverage in daily newspapers, magazines, and wire services
- get on radio and television

BECOME A MEDIA WATCHER

If you aren't one already, you should become an avid media watcher. The sooner you do so, the better prepared you'll be when it comes time to launch your publicity campaign. Read as many newspapers as possible to see who is covering what. Take note of stories that relate to your organization's sphere of activities and write down where they appear and whose byline they carry. Watch the editorial pages, op-ed columns, and "Letters to the Editor" as well. All are possible outlets for publicity. Keeping a list or card file of names will give you a leg up when it comes time to develop a media list.

Television and radio news and talk shows are other possible outlets. Become familiar with their formats. Find volunteers who are willing to monitor such programs and write short evaluations of their style and content for your files. Not only will this kind of research tip you off as to which shows might be appropriate forums for your message, it will also provide you with clues as to what kinds of stories appeal to their producers and audiences.

CREATING A PUBLICITY CAMPAIGN

Publicity should be incorporated into your organization's overall public relations agenda. At the same time, each publicity campaign requires a specific plan that identifies who your primary audiences are, what you hope to accomplish, and the best method for communicating your message.

Take the example of a community group that wants to release a report on the conditions of the city's day-care centers. Its objective is to garner as much publicity for the report as possible in order to move the local government to vote new funds for day care. The audiences it needs to reach to accomplish that objective include school administrators, parents, teachers, and local politicians (i.e., the mayor, town supervisor, and various county officials). Once the group has identified its objectives and audiences, it can create a strategy for carrying out its plan. Such a strategy should pinpoint the kind of publicity the group seeks—whether from hard news stories, features, editorials, and/or interviews—while specifying how different messages will be used to reach different audiences. (On occasion, different messages for different audiences will overlap.)

A publicity campaign need not focus on a specific event or a single objective. Take, for example, a technology institute that prepares college-age kids for high-tech careers—we'll call it John Jones College—which is interested in attracting higher quality students. Its campaign outlines specific objectives designed to help it achieve its overall goal; in turn, each objective calls for a number of different strategies. Example 4 outlines a portion of the publicity plan for John Jones College.

"Once the group has identified its objectives and audiences, it can create a strategy for carrying out its [publicity] plan."

Example 4. Publicity Plan for John Jones College

Objective	Audience	Media Relations Program
Promote John Jones as a quality academic institution	Parents, high school teachers and administrators; guidance counselors; alumni, current students, and faculty; administrators at sister institutions	Arrange background meetings with key educational reporters and representatives from editorial boards; develop potential feature-story angles for placement in print and electronic media; invite media to cover institutional open house
Promote John Jones' career education program and fine placement record	Parents, high school students, guidance counselors, industry groups, corporate personnel departments	Attempt to publicize John Jones' career approach to education among career columnists at major metropolitan dailies; use reprints in mailings to guidance counselors and teachers, and as handouts at appropriate college fairs

Example 4. Publicity Plan for John Jones College (continued)

Objective	Audience	Media Relations Program
Promote John Jones as one of the country's leading research centers in computer graphics, lasers, robotics, optics, etc.	Industry groups, corporate personnel departments, scientific organizations	Introduce John Jones' programs and spokespersons to reporters at appropriate business publications (e.g., *Forbes, Business Week, Fortune, The Wall Street Journal*).

In addition to specific objectives, audiences, messages, and strategies, a publicity plan must include a budget and timeline. These last two elements will help you decide what is possible—and what is not. Example 5 shows a typical timeline for the media component of an open house.

Although preparing a detailed plan can be time-consuming, it's almost always worth the effort. A detailed plan will help you keep your publicity campaign under control, aid you in delegating tasks equitably, and allow you to establish clear deadlines for support staff and volunteers.

Once such a plan is developed, a comprehensive media list and materials targeted for the media should be assembled.

Example 5. Target Event: Institutional Open House, Seven-Week Campaign

Week	Media Kit Folder	Media Advisory on Event
1st week	Meet with designer of media kit cover	
2nd week	Assemble background materials, brochures, annual reports, etc.	
3rd week	Mechanical prepared by designer; send to printer for kit labels	Media list assembled and put on labels/envelopes
4th week	Draft insert materials for kit (news release, program, backgrounder on school, opening address, biographies)	Media advisory drafted, edited, approved, sent to print shop
5th week	Receive folders from printer	Media advisory from print shop
6th week	Offset insert materials	Advisory mailed to media; begin follow-up calls to all media invited to cover event
7th week	Stuff and label	Complete follow-up calls to media

DEVELOPING A MEDIA LIST

An important element of any publicity campaign is a comprehensive media list—that is, the names and addresses of all the journalists and broadcasters you plan to approach during the campaign. Along with names and addresses, media lists should include telephone numbers and, when available, fax numbers and e-mail addresses.

The kinds of media and media contacts incorporated into any list should include the following:

- national daily newspapers
- local and regional newspapers
- wire services and syndicates
- newsweeklies
- consumer publications
- Sunday supplements
- trade publications
- cable outlets
- columnists
- television news and news magazine producers

When compiling a media list, keep in mind the following points:

- There is a difference between a comprehensive media mailing list and a list tailored for a specific campaign.
- Board, staff, and volunteers should be canvassed for the names of media contacts.
- Media outlets should always be examined with the audiences you want to reach and the messages you hope to communicate in mind.

Sources for obtaining the names of reporters and editors can be found in the Media Resources list on page 58.

Metropolitan Dailies

There are approximately 8,100 newspapers in the United States—about 1,590 dailies and nearly 6,500 weekly, bi-weekly, or tri-weekly newspapers—according to *Editor & Publisher International Yearbook*.

Among these are several dailies that are considered national news outlets. These include *The New York Times*, *The Washington Post*, the

> "... media lists should include telephone numbers and, when available, fax numbers and e-mail addresses."

Los Angeles Times, the *Chicago Tribune,* the *Christian Science Monitor,* and *USA Today.* Although its news focus is business-oriented, *The Wall Street Journal* is also considered a national daily. A national daily should only be approached when a story has national implications or affects the city where the paper is published.

In addition to national dailies, every major metropolitan market has at least one morning or evening daily that covers local and national news. Most dailies get the majority of their national stories from the wire services and generate local and regional stories with their own reporters.

The key to a successful publicity campaign that utilizes daily newspapers is knowing what editors want and how to give it to them. Most dailies actually consist of a number of specialized sections (e.g., metropolitan, business, sports, arts, lifestyle), departments (e.g., "Letters to the Editor," the op-ed page), and listings (e.g., social calendar, classifieds, obituaries, TV listings). Each section usually has its own editor and staff and should be approached accordingly.

Different editors will be interested in different angles. A story on volunteerism, for example, may be right for the business section if it illustrates how nonprofit organizations muster resources from the private sector. The lifestyle editor may use similar material if it provides an in-depth look at a socially prominent volunteer's motivation. Whatever the angle, try to pitch your story to the reporter or desk most likely to be interested in that particular subject or angle.

Deadlines for daily papers vary, depending on whether the story is "hard" or "soft" news. Hard news is immediate—for example, a story with the headline PLANE SHOT DOWN IN CUBA—and can be turned around quickly. Soft news has no timeline—as in a story with the headline ESTHER SMITH, A VOLUNTEER OF EXTRAORDINARY NOTE—and generally requires a longer lead time. The hard news deadline for most morning papers falls on the afternoon of the day *before* publication; deadlines for afternoon papers are in the morning.

"The key to a successful publicity campaign that utilizes daily newspapers is knowing what editors want and how to give it to them."

Columnists

There is a school of thought which holds that journalists who cover a particular area or "beat"—for example, social service, religion, or the arts—are happy to receive any and every report from organizations working in the field. Certainly, special-interest editors and columnists should be included on your media list. Get to know who covers the issues and topics of concern to your organization at the dailies and weeklies in your region as well as at the major dailies around the country.

Many columnists also have their work syndicated nationally. To find out which columnists freelance and which ones are affiliated with a particular paper, consult one of the several media guides listed at the end of this section.

WHO'S WHO ON A NEWSPAPER STAFF

- Assignment editors make judgments regarding which stories should be covered by which reporters and photographers.

- Department editors are responsible for handling news within their given area or field of expertise.

- City editors handle news of interest to people living and/or working in the city where the paper is published; they may assign a reporter to cover a specific event.

- Special-section editors are responsible for items that appear in particular weekly or Sunday sections.

- Editorial page editors are responsible for a paper's editorial page and "Letters to the Editor" department; op-ed page editors should receive manuscripts intended for the op-ed page.

- Columnists are responsible for the material that appears in their columns.

- Calendar and listings editors handle announcements of special events, fundraising benefits, community activities, and the like.

(Note: If you send a release to more than one reporter at a newspaper, make sure all the recipients are carbon-copied.)

Sunday Editions and Supplements

Most major dailies publish larger—and sometimes voluminous—Sunday editions with special sections for national and local news, features, arts and culture, real estate, business, and television listings. Usually, each section has its own editorial staff. In addition, many Sunday editions carry magazine supplements such as *Parade,* which has its own editorial staff and offices. A few of the large-circulation dailies even publish their own Sunday magazines, which, like their other Sunday sections, have a separate editorial staff. You should familiarize yourself with these kinds of publications to determine whether their editors are likely to be interested in a story. And, when planning a publicity campaign, keep in mind the fact that Sunday supplements have long lead times.

Weekly Newspapers

For the most part, weekly newspapers are locally based operations. To appear in a weekly, a story usually must have a local news hook or appeal. As a result, it's often easier to garner exposure in a weekly than in a daily. Plan to have your story ready further in advance, however, as most weeklies have small staffs and require a longer lead time. To find out who the editors and reporters at your local weekly are, consult a local media directory or simply call the paper and ask.

Newsweeklies

Time, Newsweek, and *U.S. News & World Report* report on events of national and international importance. Published every Monday, all three have a Friday deadline, although some departments close earlier in the week. And at all three, it's not unusual for several writers and editors to contribute to a single article, drawing on information collected from news bureaus around the nation and the globe.

Publicists should cultivate relationships with editors at newsweeklies as appropriate. Newsweeklies, like national dailies, have regional news bureaus whose reporters often initiate stories of particular interest to their region or locale. For organizations outside Washington, D.C., or New York (where all the large-circulation newsweeklies are based), it's often easier and more efficient to contact a regional bureau than to try to go through a magazine's national office.

Consumer Magazines

Mass-circulation magazines such as *Vogue, Cosmopolitan, Reader's Digest, TV Guide, Vanity Fair, Esquire, GQ, Prevention,* and *ArtNews* appeal to a wide variety of audiences. If you plan to use one or more of them in a publicity campaign, select your target publications carefully.

Which publications do your supporters or potential supporters read? What do they think of the publications they don't read? How does a magazine fit into your overall public relations objectives? Always look for the magazine whose readers are most important to your organization; then begin to make contacts.

Start with a telephone call to a specific editor or a writer who contributes frequently to that magazine to discuss a story idea. Many of the large-circulation monthlies work three to four months ahead of publication and guard their editorial plans zealously. By developing individual relationships with key editors and freelance writers who are constantly pitching their own stories, a publicist increases his or her chances of becoming a valued source for story ideas while raising the "profile" of the organization or cause he or she represents.

"Always look for the magazine whose readers are most important to your organization; then begin to make contacts."

Trade Media

The term *trade media* describes professional and specialty print and electronic media outlets that deal with specific industries and interests. For instance, *Dance Magazine* covers the dance world; *Advertising Age* and *AdWeek* cover the advertising industry. Although such outlets are usually thought of in terms of straight news, they also offer placement opportunities for bylined or feature articles. Because they differ enormously in format, however, you should read and review several issues of the publication you've targeted in order to obtain a better understanding of what kind of news item or feature story appeals to its editors. Again, it's important to check publication deadlines, since many trade publications work months in advance.

Because they tend to be short-staffed and short of funds, the less well-known and smaller-circulation publications and newsletters often will pick up news releases and submitted photos with little or no alteration. As always, the strength of the materials and the credibility of the source figure greatly in whether or not trade media will give you the exposure you desire.

Wire Services

Rather than supply materials of national interest to hundreds of daily and weekly newspapers, it is sometimes more cost-efficient and effective to supply a few select news syndicates or wire services with such information. The better-known wire services include the Associated Press (AP), United Press International (UPI), and Reuters. Each service has writers who cover specific topics or areas of interest in addition to editors who deal with special kinds of stories—much like a daily newspaper.

Both UPI and the AP maintain a national wire, which carries stories of national importance, and state wires, which carry items of state and regional significance. The national wire is often referred to as the *A wire;* state wires are called *B wires.*

Wire-service editors look for stories that will serve their subscriber newspapers. Just because an editor decides a story is newsworthy and runs it on the wire is no guarantee that it will appear in print, however. For that reason, it is sometimes advisable to send your news item or story to individual newspapers as well as to the wire services. For example, if the purpose of a publicity plan is to inform legislators in the state capital, give your information to the wire as well as to the major newspapers in the capital.

In some cities the wire services maintain daily listings of upcoming events, special programs, and the comings and goings of public officials, foreign dignitaries, and the like. Called *daybooks,* these listings of potentially newsworthy events are wired to subscribers every afternoon so that editors can plan reporting assignments in advance. Daybook editors will often include information about newsworthy events and programs in their listings if they receive written notice several days in advance. If the story has a visual component, contact the wire service's photo editor and invite a photographer to cover the event.

You should cultivate wire-service editors and beat reporters the same way you cultivate your daily media contacts. Know their requirements, interests, working habits, and deadlines. To find the local address of a wire service, start with the phone book. The major wire services have bureaus in most big cities, and their *stringers*—field reporters who take on specific assignments—can be found virtually everywhere.

> "*You should cultivate wire-service editors and beat reporters the same way you cultivate your daily media contacts.*"

Syndicates

In addition to the news wires, there are a variety of other services and syndicates, ranging from the National Catholic News Service, which provides news and feature stories to the Catholic Diocesan media, to the Dow Jones News Service, which traffics in business news. There's even a PR Newswire, which sends press releases for distribution by computer link to newspapers around the country. (Unlike the others, PR Newswire is a paid distribution service.)

There are, in addition, a variety of feature syndicates (about 400) that distribute news features, columns, cartoons, editorials, and *mats* (camera- or press-ready copy). Most are strictly journalistic organizations with writers and columnists servicing papers around the country.

Similarly, photo syndicates distribute photos to subscriber newspapers and, increasingly, online news services. Among the better-known photo syndicates are AP/Worldwide Photos, Associated Press Newsphotos, Reuters News Pictures, and United Press International Newspictures. However, while thousands of pictures a day are submitted to these syndicates, only a few are chosen for distribution. Photo syndicates also will assign photographers to cover specific events, although there's no guarantee the resulting photos will be used. In most cases, you should query the syndicate first to ascertain its interest.

Television and Radio

A television and radio media list should consist of the names of:

- assignment editors at network and national cable TV stations
- assignment editors at appropriate local TV, cable, and radio stations
- producers and talent coordinators (people who book guests) at television and radio talk shows
- producers of public-affairs and community-related programming
- producers of television news magazine shows

The addition of audio and visual components and the instantaneous transmission of those components make television and radio reporting different from print media. But as any media watcher soon learns, TV and radio often take their lead from the print media. As a result, alerting TV and radio stations to an item in the newspapers can result in welcome publicity.

Television and radio offer a host of publicity possibilities. In addition to their regularly scheduled newscasts, most television and radio stations are required by law to create and air community-related public-affairs programming. Such programming runs the gamut from local or regional newsmaker programs and panel discussions of public-health issues to simple listings of area cultural events. Much of this programming relies on a low-budget "talking heads" format and usually airs on Sunday morning or late at night. Still, this kind of programming can get the word out. Although they may not be large by prime-time standards, public-affairs programs usually have audiences numbering in the thousands.

Outside the public-affairs arena, there are a growing number of television shows, including such morning programs as "Good Morning America" and "The Today Show" and evening news magazines like "Prime Time Live" and "Dateline," that offer opportunities for issue-oriented interviews and/or mention in special reports featuring taped interviews with experts on thematic issues. To get on a network TV or

". . . as any media watcher soon learns, TV and radio often take their lead from the print media."

MEDIA RESOURCES

A media list can also be created by consulting a number of media directories. A list of some of the better-known directories follows:

- *Bacon's Publicity Checker* publishes the names of department editors at daily and weekly newspapers nationwide. It also publishes a magazine list, organized by specialty category and industry group, with the names of key editors. An annual subscription entitles the subscriber to periodic updates.

- *The News Media Yellow Book of Washington, D.C., and New York* is a comprehensive listing of news media, including newspapers, network affiliates and local TV stations, local cable stations, radio stations, news services, periodicals, newsletters, publishers, foreign media, and syndicated columnists.

- *The Broadcasting and Cable Yearbook* has information about television, cable, and radio stations, their formats, and the names of top staff.

- *California Publicity Outlets* surveys West Coast media outlets.

- *Editor & Publisher International Yearbook* provides complete contact information for hundreds of domestic and foreign newspapers.

- *Hudson's Washington Media* lists Washington, D.C.-based media, including local bureaus across the country.

- *New York Publicity Outlets* surveys a variety of print and broadcast media outlets, both local and national in scope, based in New York City and the greater metropolitan area.

- *TV Publicity Outlets* provides a national listing of news-oriented television programs.

- *Radio Publicity Outlets* offers a national listing of news-oriented radio talk shows. It also provides a wealth of information on station formats.

In addition, there are any number of reliable and up-to-date media directories for major metropolitan areas around the country. Consult a local publicity club or press association for the names of those that cover your area.

cable program, however, the story must be a visual one. "Talking heads" are of little interest to the producers of weekly television news magazines, who, instead, are always on the lookout for good visual material that helps tell a story.

There are dozens of radio stations—AM and FM—in any given listening area, and most program some kind of news, talk, or listener call-in component. Since guests often aren't listed for these kinds of programs, you almost have to become a regular listener to determine whether your organization, cause, or issue is a match for the program's focus and format.

MEDIA MATERIALS

> "It has been said that the difference between an amateur and a professional publicist is that the amateur thinks of his story while the professional thinks of his audience. Judge your own news release by asking, 'Would this interest me?' If the answer is no, start again."
> —Leona Pappas, "Big Ideas Publicity,"
> from the Broadcast Promotion Association

Nonprofits are in the news every day, commissioning and releasing studies, announcing new or unique programs, celebrating successful fundraising campaigns, hiring new staff, and commenting on current events. Often, they are linked to stories that are timely or involve famous people or large amounts of money—or both. Nonprofits make news simply because what they do often affects large numbers of people. And nonprofits that are good at publicity present their stories in a variety of ways to make them attractive to the media.

". . . nonprofits that are good at publicity present their stories in a variety of ways to make them attractive to the media."

Story Angles

There are several ways to "sell" your story or event to the media—even if it isn't what is called "hard news."

Let's assume that a community service group has developed programs for young children, families, and the elderly in a particular neighborhood. These programs include counseling services for housing, legal, and financial problems; employment counseling; and a number of services such as school-lunch and day-care programs. At best, the activities of the center present possibilities for a number of feature stories—"soft," rather than "hard," news stories.

How do you get local media to write about the center? First, think like an editor. What are the possible stories that might be developed about the center? In this instance, story angles might include:

- portraits of the neighborhood elderly and how the center helps them
- what it's like to grow old in the neighborhood
- the difficulties faced by young people growing up in the neighborhood
- a story about "the business of helping"
- a profile of a particularly effective or successful program
- a story about how a program has made a difference in the life of a neighborhood resident
- a "day in the life" story about a center employee
- a profile of the center's director
- mini-profiles of various center volunteers

Researching the value of and substance behind an idea allows a good publicist to assemble sufficient material to make a story attractive to the largest number of media outlets.

News Releases

After selecting a number of story ideas and deciding who should receive publicity materials and within what time frame, the next step is to prepare your materials. There are several types of news release, each with its own style and possibilities. Examples of each type and instructions for their preparation follow:

Hard News Release. A straight news story, such as the announcement of personnel changes, a new grant, an important new study, or a performance or benefit, can be communicated in a hard news release. Hard news releases are characterized by their quick pace and brevity. (See pages 62–70 for examples.)

Feature Release. A feature release takes the news peg and gives it a human interest twist. Features can be profiles, stories about individuals' or organizations' successes, eloquent waxing (within limits) about an organization's community contributions, or slices of life that dramatize a particular group's contribution. No matter how "soft" the story, however, it should be timely and have some relevance to a topic in the news.

"No matter how 'soft' the story . . . it should be timely and have some relevance to a topic in the news."

The Backgrounder. Backgrounders provide explanatory information that can be used in follow-up stories. They can be designed to provoke an editor, fill in some blanks, or simply be filed as a resource. They can also be prepared and packaged with other, more timely materials. But they should be brief—no more than two single-spaced pages.

Fact Sheets. Fact sheets serve much the same purpose as backgrounders. They can be prepared in advance and sent quickly when the occasion arises or included with other materials in response to a question or inquiry. For example, your organization may have reached a point where it is receiving a steady stream of inquiries about its funding, structure, history, awards, and accomplishments. The answers to these and similar questions can be part of a fact sheet. Fact sheets on organizational issues and topics should be updated as needed. Although they require a certain amount of research and legwork, they are extremely useful for keeping your media contacts informed and the "voice" of your organization consistent. (See pages 71–72 for an example.)

Question-and-Answer Sheet (Q&A). Q&As are abbreviated fact sheets prepared in question-and-answer format. Some reporters prefer Q&As to backgrounders.

Biographies. Biographies are used to provide data on key spokespeople within an organization. They are usually one to two pages in length and summarize a person's experience and significant achievements. (See page 73 for an example.)

Media Advisories and Media Alerts. These aim to do just what their name indicates—that is, advise or alert various media outlets about an event or story. The most effective examples of the form function like an invitation, with a format to match. In other words, be sure to include in brief outline form the what, when, where, and who of the event or story you want to publicize. (See page 74 for an example.)

News Kits. News kits usually consist of an assortment of materials placed in folders and sent to various media contacts as a way of familiarizing those contacts with an organization and its programs. They can be modest or lavish, depending on the amount and type of materials being sent and your objectives in sending them, but they should provide all the information an editor or producer will need to create a story, including background and biographical material. A news kit can contain any or all of the following:

- a news release with a release date. Each release should be a self-contained item, listing the name and telephone

"Fact sheets on organizational issues . . . are extremely useful for keeping your media contacts informed and the 'voice' of your organization consistent."

innovations
IN STATE AND LOCAL GOVERNMENT
N E W S

An awards program
of the Ford Foundation
and Harvard University

Contact: Karen Borack/Alex Paidas   Lloyd Garrison
              M Booth & Associates   Ford Foundation
              212/481-7000   212/573-4925

EMBARGOED FOR RELEASE - A.M. PAPERS
Thursday, September 29, 1994

MASSACHUSETTS'S SCORE PROJECT NAMED WINNER OF
1994 INNOVATIONS IN STATE AND LOCAL GOVERNMENT AWARD

Initiative to Receive a $100,000 Ford Foundation Grant

NEW YORK, N.Y., September 29, 1994--Massachusetts's SCORE (Student Conflict
Resolution Experts) program, which trains students in urban schools to act as mediators to
help their peers resolve violent conflicts peacefully, has been named a winner of a 1994
Innovations in State and Local Government Award by the Ford Foundation and the John
F. Kennedy School of Government at Harvard University. The state program will receive
a $100,000 grant from the Foundation at a Washington, D.C. ceremony tonight.

Considered to be among the nation's most prestigious public service awards, the
Innovations Program recognizes novel efforts at the state and local levels that are unusually
successful in addressing public needs. The 10 award-winners were selected from a pool of
nearly 1,300 applications from jurisdictions nationwide.

The Ford grant will be used by SCORE to disseminate and replicate the program.
Plans include hosting a national conference for law enforcement and education officials,
conducting training sessions and regional workshops for schools, creating new curriculum
materials for chronically violent youth, and establishing a training institute to increase the
number of teachers qualified to train student mediators.

(MORE)

Innovations Program
John F. Kennedy School of Government
A. Alfred Taubman Center
79 John F. Kennedy Street
Cambridge, MA 02138

-2-

"The 1994 Innovations Award recipients reflect the creative thinking of dedicated public employees who are attempting to make government work better for all people," said Franklin A. Thomas, president of the Ford Foundation. "As state and local governments play increasingly important roles in improving the quality of our lives, we are glad to honor projects that show government at its most creative."

SCORE is a statewide effort to teach youths, many of whom are themselves at risk of dropping out of school or displaying violent behavior, skills in resolving conflicts in nonviolent ways and to enlist them to use these skills to help their peers reduce or eliminate violence through mediation. A second prong of the program, Conflict Intervention Teams (CITs), enables trained teams of adult and student mediators to intervene when schoolwide outbreaks of violence, such as those involving racially motivated conflicts, close or threaten to close a school.

Administered by the Massachusetts Attorney General, who strongly supports prevention efforts as a way of reducing urban violence, SCORE began in 1989 as a two-year pilot project in two high schools. As of mid-1994, SCORE programs were operating in 13 high schools and seven middle schools across Massachusetts. To date, more than 700 students have gone through SCORE's 20-hour mediation training course, and 75 adult and student mediators have participated on CITs.

(MORE)

-3-

SCORE relies on referrals from administrators and teachers to alert the mediators when tense situations arise. Since its inception, SCORE has mediated more than 2,500 disputes, with about 97 percent resulting in agreements. To date, less than 5 percent had been breached after one year.

"In our search for 'silver bullet' solutions to crime and violence, we often overlook our obligation to address the underlying causes of these problems," said Massachusetts Attorney General Scott Harshbarger. "SCORE is a concrete and cost-effective response to the root of crime and violence."

The program is funded not with taxpayers' dollars, but with money raised through negotiated settlements with businesses that have been charged with violating the state's consumer protection laws.

Since 1986 the Ford Foundation has granted $8.9 million to 125 exemplary projects in the Innovations Program. This year the award-winning programs, chosen from among 25 finalists, represent governmental units in six states, two cities, one county, and one school district.

On July 15, officials representing the finalists made presentations to a national selection committee at the Kennedy School in Cambridge, Mass. In addition to the $100,000 to each of the 10 winners, the Ford Foundation will grant $20,000 to each of the 15 other finalists.

(MORE)

-4-

Four criteria were used to evaluate each program: its novelty; its effectiveness in addressing important local or national problems; the value of the service it provides to clients; and the degree to which it can be replicated.

The National Committee on Innovations in State and Local Government, chaired by William G. Milliken, former Governor of Michigan, selected the 10 winners and 15 finalists.

Other members of the National Committee are:

Margaret Gordon, dean, Graduate School of Public Affairs at the University of Washington

Antonia Hernandez, president and general counsel, Mexican American Legal Defense and Educational Fund

Luis G. Nogales, chairman and chief executive officer, Embarcadero Media, Inc.

Dorothy S. Ridings, publisher and president, The Bradenton (Florida) Herald

Jack Rosenthal, assistant managing editor, The New York Times

Ellen Schall, professor, Robert F. Wagner School of Public Service at New York University

Max R. Sherman, dean, Lyndon B. Johnson School of Public Affairs at the University of Texas

Hubert Williams, president, Police Foundation

Harriett Ruth Woods, president, National Women's Political Caucus

Andrew Young, co-chair, Atlanta Committee for the Olympic Games.

(MORE)

-5-

The Innovations Program is directed by Professor Alan Altshuler of the A. Alfred Taubman Center for State and Local Government at Harvard's John F. Kennedy School of Government.

The John F. Kennedy School of Government is one of the nation's foremost schools of public affairs. Its mission is to train leaders for excellence in government and public service and to foster understanding of major public issues.

The Ford Foundation, established in 1936, is a private, nonprofit institution that serves as a resource for innovative people and institutions worldwide. Its goals are to strengthen democratic values, reduce poverty and injustice, promote international cooperation, and advance human achievement. A national and international philanthropy with an endowment of $6.5 billion, the Foundation has granted more than $8 billion to recipients worldwide. The Foundation maintains headquarters in New York City and has offices in 17 countries in Africa, Asia, and Latin America.

Brief descriptions of the 10 Innovations Award-winners are attached.

####

Local Contact: Ed Cafasso
                            Director of Communications
                            Office of the Attorney General
                            617/727-2543

THE WOODROW WILSON
NATIONAL FELLOWSHIP FOUNDATION

Haskell Rhett
President

Contact: Emily Whitfield/Beth Chute   FOR IMMEDIATE RELEASE
           (212) 481-7000

FEDERAL MANAGERS FEAR DOWNSIZING COULD
DEVASTATE DIVERSITY INITIATIVES IN FEDERAL AGENCIES

Washington, D.C.-- February 11, 1994. Responding to growing concerns that government downsizing will harm diversity initiatives, managers from six federal agencies today formed a working group to consider strategies to ensure that staff freezes and layoffs do not derail minority hiring and promotion in the federal workforce.

The working group, citing recent reports of persistent failures to retain and promote minorities, believes that pressures to reduce staffing at all levels could further reduce the ranks of minorities in the federal workforce. According to reports by the Equal Employment Opportunity Commission (EEOC), top-level managers in most federal agencies are at least 90 percent white, and the numbers of minorities entering the middle and top ranks is declining. Blacks and Hispanics in particular are concentrated among the lower grades of the civil service.

"Race continues to define who governs, despite a generation of equal opportunity goal-setting by policymakers and educators," said Dr. Allan E. Goodman, a convener of the group and Associate Dean and Director of Georgetown University's Graduate School of Foreign Service. "The formation of this working group is evidence of a persistent problem. Hopefully, the current administration will contribute a significant part of an enduring solution."

(more)

CN 5281 • Princeton, NJ 08543-5281 • Telephone: (609) 452-7007 • Facsimile: (609) 452-0066
Delivery Address: 5 Vaughn Drive • Suite 300 • Princeton, NJ 08540-6313

- 2 -

The working group drew together participants from the Department of Education, Department of Commerce, Department of Defense, Department of State, National Security Council and Office of Personnel Management.

"Increasing diversity is not just a numbers game," said Ernest J. Wilson III, Staff Member at the National Security Council. "Given the direction of the world around us -- and given the direction of the country -- it produces better public policy for all Americans." Minorities -- African Americans, Hispanics, Asian Americans and Native Americans -- are expected to comprise one-third of the population by the year 2000. Yet according to the EEOC's latest assessment of future prospects, underrepresentation for all minorities at managerial grade levels is projected to continue through the end of the century, while underrepresentation of federal Hispanic employees is actually widening. "From the top levels on down, I sense a willingness to change assumptions," said John Hall, Director of Personnel at the U.S. Department of State. "There's an awful lot of smoke here -- there's got to be a fire."

As a call to action, the working group outlined an agenda to counter any backsliding caused by staffing reductions. Strategies include:

.   developing pressure groups inside government agencies to promote
     hiring and promotion of African Americans, Hispanics, Asian
     Americans and Native Americans;

.   boosting minority hiring in those select areas where government is
     growing, e.g., the FDA and the Department of Education;

(more)

- 3 -

- opening a dialogue with higher-level decision makers agency-wide about fostering programs to hire and promote minorities;

- encouraging mentoring through minority advocacy groups for public policy professionals;

- addressing the "glass ceiling" problem by organizing professional development seminars; and

- steering high school programs to the college and graduate-level pipeline for minorities to enter public policy and international affairs careers.

In the search for solutions, managers recognized two existing programs that have been successful in promoting diversity. Within government, managers cited the leadership of the Thursday Luncheon Group (TLG). Led by minority professionals in the Department of State and funded by DOS, TLG hosts regular luncheons with guest speakers, and supports mentoring and professional development through continuing education seminars, as well as Federal Women's Leadership and High School Outreach programs.

In higher education, the Woodrow Wilson National Fellowship Program in Public Policy and International Affairs is the first large-scale, successful program to offer a direct pipeline of highly qualified, minority graduate students to the public and private sector. Managers agreed that this sort of program should be replicated throughout higher education and government institutions.

(more)

- 4 -

"The inadequacy of direct support for persons of color to pursue advanced degrees reflects the way in which our society and its institutions funds such initiatives," said Dr. Richard O. Hope, Vice President of the Woodrow Wilson National Fellowship Foundation. "Over the past decade and longer, it has been private foundations -- rather than the federal government -- that have kept many programs alive."

"The current administration is open, perhaps more so now than in the past, to addressing the issue of diversity in government in meaningful terms," said Dr. Allan E. Goodman. "We must act now to keep open this window of opportunity, especially at a time when general downsizing could have further detrimental effects on efforts to close the gap."

# # #

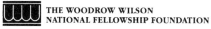

THE WOODROW WILSON
NATIONAL FELLOWSHIP FOUNDATION

Haskell Rhett
President

Contact: Emily Whitfield/Beth Chute
             (212) 481-7000

**Facts About The Woodrow Wilson National Fellowship Program
in Public Policy and International Affairs**

The Woodrow Wilson National Fellowship Program in Public Policy and International Affairs (PPIA) identifies and trains minorities for careers in public service.

The program, an effort to narrow the gap between whites and minorities in public service at all levels, selects highly qualified minority students to help increase the supply of minorities to graduate schools, and eventually jobs in the public sector.

It annually identifies minority students -- especially those from "at risk" groups in society -- and enables them to pursue graduate degrees in public policy or international affairs. Of the approximately 30 programs nationwide that advance opportunities in graduate education for minorities, PPIA is by far the largest in terms of the number of students reached and scholarship funds granted.

In addition to providing scholarship funds in the form of stipends and grants for graduate school, PPIA also provides funding for summer skill-building workshops, internships, and other costs related to the program's training.

o   PPIA annually selects 150 African American, Hispanic, Asian American, and Native American college students in their junior year to enter the program.

o   Once selected, PPIA guides students through the process of applying to and matriculating in graduate school. The **Junior Year Summer Institute** is a seven- to eight-week study program during the summer after junior year in college that provides them with substantive knowledge and analytical skills, helps with graduate school applications, counsels and monitors their progress through undergraduate school, and gives graduate schools an early assessment of their abilities. The **Senior Year Summer Program** meets the different needs of students entering graduate school by offering quantitative courses, language training, and internships. A **Graduate Fellowship** is awarded to students who complete the Junior Year Summer Institute and are accepted by a graduate school -- it includes complete funding for the first year, and funding for the second year based on financial need.

CN 5281 • Princeton, NJ 08543-5281 • Telephone (609) 452-7007 • Facsimile (609) 452-0066
Delivery Address: 5 Vaughn Drive • Suite 300 • Princeton, NJ 08540-6313

o   Other components of PPIA include **Pairing Programs,** which link undergraduate schools with large minority enrollments to universities that have established graduate public policy and international affairs programs. In the past, PPIA also has funded a limited number of **Ph.D. Fellowships** for fellows who wish to study for a Ph.D. in economics, political science, or international relations as a route to a career in international affairs. There are several Ph.D. fellows currently studying for advanced degrees.

o   Since 1989, 804 minority students have been selected as Woodrow Wilson Fellows. The majority of these fellows have attended the nation's most prestigious graduate schools and programs.

o   Thirty-two graduate schools and programs at universities throughout the U.S. participate in PPIA.

o   In many of the participating graduate schools, Woodrow Wilson Fellows account for between 25 and 50 percent of all minority students.

o   Woodrow Wilson Fellows successfully gain employment in a wide variety of public service jobs as well as in highly competitive fields in the private sector.

# # #

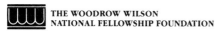

THE WOODROW WILSON
NATIONAL FELLOWSHIP FOUNDATION

Haskell Rhett
President

Contact: Emily Whitfield/Beth Chute
(212) 481-7000

BIOGRAPHICAL SKETCH

ALLAN E. GOODMAN

Allan E. Goodman is Associate Dean for Graduate Studies at Georgetown University's School of Foreign Service and Professor of International Affairs.

An expert on the theory and practice of international negotiation and forecasting for strategic planning, he also conducts specialized research on intelligence problems and systems and their influence on U.S. foreign relations.

Prior to coming to Georgetown in 1980, Dr. Goodman served as Presidential Briefing Coordinator for the Director of Central Intelligence and as Special Assistant to the Director of the National Foreign Assessment Center in the Carter Administration. He was Chairman of the Department of Government and International Relations at Clark University (1971-1974) and a National Fellow at Stanford University's Hoover Institution (1974-1975).

Dr. Goodman is a member of the board of advisors of the Pew Faculty Fellowship Program at Harvard University and the editorial board of Asian Survey, published at the University of California, Berkeley. He serves as a consultant to the Ford and Woodrow Wilson National Fellowship Foundations on increasing the representation of minorities in public policy and international affairs careers.

Dr. Goodman is the author of more than 100 books, chapters, and articles on international affairs. His most recent book is A Brief History of the Future (Westview Press), and he is the editor of the forthcoming Diplomatic Record, 1992-1993. His recent articles focus on prospects for the normalization of U.S.-Vietnam relations.

In 1991, he was awarded a Doctor of Laws, honoris causa, from Mount Ida College. He is a frequent guest on the Voice of America's "Encounter" program, which is broadcast to 120 million listeners worldwide.

Dr. Goodman received a B.S. with honors in 1966 from Northwestern University, M.P.A. in 1968 from the John F. Kennedy School of Government, Harvard University, and Ph.D. in 1971 from the Department of Government, Harvard University.

# # #

CN 5281 • Princeton, NJ 08543-5281 • Telephone (609) 452-7007 • Facsimile (609) 452-0066
Delivery Address: 5 Vaughn Drive • Suite 300 • Princeton, NJ 08540-6313

PROJECT RETURN FOUNDATION, INC.
A FAMILY OF PROGRAMS SERVING THE FAMILY OF MAN

Contact: Karen Borack 212/481-7000
            Julio Cotto   212/979-8800

For Immediate Release

* * * MEDIA ALERT * * *

PHOTO OPPORTUNITY

**PAROLEES GIVE CHRISTMAS GIFT OF THEMSELVES TO TODDLERS AND THEIR MOMS
WHO ARE STRIVING TO OVERCOME DRUG AND EMOTIONAL PROBLEMS**

Project Return Clients Share Christmas Joy at Holiday Party

WHAT: Residents of Project Return's Transitional Treatment Program will host a Holiday
            Party for women and their young children living at the Project Return Albert and
            Mildred Dreitzer Women & Children's Treatment Center. The men will play
            Santa Claus, give toys and sing carols.

WHO: Men on parole who have been incarcerated for drug related violations

            Toddlers and their mothers who are living in a therapeutic residential setting to
            overcome drug and psychological problems

WHEN: Tuesday, December 13
            5:30 PM to 8 PM

WHERE: Project Return Transitional Treatment Center
            2112 Second Avenue (between 108 and 109 Street) - Manhattan
            Ground Floor

BACKGROUND: The Project Return Foundation offers an array of services for substance
            abusers to help them live independent and productive lives. The Albert and
            Mildred Dreitzer Children's Center is a unique approach that allows women with
            a dual diagnosis of substance abuse and mental illness to stay with their young
            children while they work toward recovery. The Transitional Treatment Program
            is a residential structured therapeutic program for parolees with substance
            abuse problems.

                            ####

10 ASTOR PLACE, NEW YORK, NY 10003-6935 ▪ (212) 979-8800 ▪ FAX (212) 979-0100

number of a contact person authorized to provide additional information to the media.

- a feature release providing a "soft" angle to the story in question;
- an organizational fact sheet;
- background material on your organization and/or the issue you wish to publicize;
- biographical information about key organization personnel;
- a question-and-answer sheet providing additional information;
- photographs (black-and-white only) that relate directly to the news item or issue you are publicizing. Photos should be full-sized (8" x 10") glossies with good contrast. Brief captions should be attached to the back or bottom of each photograph.
- brochures, catalogues, or similar material relating to your organization or the issue in question.

What to Expect and What Not to Expect from Releases and Media Materials

A survey of business editors reported in *Editor & Publisher* magazine found that only 20 percent of the respondents relied on news releases as sources of information, and that 10 percent of all editors never used them at all. Why? A majority of the respondents faulted news releases for containing irrelevant commentary (e.g., management quotes); 55 percent criticized them for burying important information; and 45 percent claimed they were poorly written.

Much of the success of a news release depends on whether it was received in a timely manner by the right person at the right outlet. Any release you issue should be newsworthy. Organizations that churn out release after release when one will do are contributing to the "little boy who cried wolf" syndrome. After a while, their releases —and sometimes those of like-minded organizations—are discarded as soon as the return address is noticed. So be selective in what you send, as well as to whom you send it.

By the same token, don't expect your releases to be used word for word; usually only certain portions of a release (e.g., quotes or factual paragraphs) are lifted verbatim. In other words, don't delay issuing a release—and risk missing your deadline—in an attempt to make it "perfect."

"Much of the success of a news release depends on whether it was received in a timely manner by the right person at the right outlet."

Writing News Releases

When it comes to writing news releases, the most important rule is: Don't editorialize. Keep your prose tight and be objective, even when writing a feature release. To put it another way: When in doubt, leave it out. Here are some additional tips for the two main types of news release, the hard news release and the feature release.

Hard News Releases. Basic journalistic practice dictates using the five Ws and the single H—*who, what, when, where, why,* and *how*—in a hard news release. Every such release should attempt to answer all six questions in the first two paragraphs. It is especially important to include the most vital information in the first paragraph, or *lead,* which should be a short (no more than 40 words) presentation of the single most newsworthy aspect of the story you are publicizing.

The classic hard news release is structured like an inverted pyramid, with less important facts, including background data and biographical information, appearing after the answers to *who, what, when, why,* and *how* are presented at the "top" of the story in its opening paragraphs. Hard news releases are formatted this way so that editors can cut material as needed from the end of the release without affecting the information that absolutely needs to be communicated. The inverted-pyramid structure also enables editors to judge the newsworthiness of a release just by reading its first few paragraphs.

As for style, the rules are simple. Be brief. Use short sentences and short paragraphs. Use the active voice as much as possible: "He announced" is more effective than "It was announced today." Make sure your release is factual and accurate and that all proper nouns are correctly spelled.

If block quotes or long lists add to the length of your release, use centered headlines and subheads to break up the blocks of copy. Headlines give an editor a quick overview of the content of a story. Longer headlines can be broken into subheads placed directly underneath the main headline:

ASPCA ANNOUNCES $2 MILLION GRANT
Completes Fundraising Campaign for New Shelters

Feature Releases. An assignment to write a feature release gives you a chance to be creative. Features can be sentimental or tongue-in-cheek, upbeat or humorous, and are constructed with an almost infinite variety of leads, from zingers and stingers to quotes and one-liners. Regardless of their tone and form, however, they should be seen as part of a whole. Feel free to experiment, but whatever you do, make sure your feature releases have an effective lead and a strong close.

"It is especially important to include the most vital information in the first paragraph, or lead. . . ."

The headline over a feature release should capture the reader's attention. A release from the U.S. Environmental Protection Agency on the effects of acid rain in one community ran under the following banner:

LOOK WHAT THEY'VE DONE TO THE RAIN, MA!

Thanks in part to the headline (which was adapted from a popular song of the '70s), the release ran in its entirety in numerous publications and generated more media attention than virtually any other release issued by the EPA over a two-year span.

The headline should be followed by an attention-grabbing lead. Make sure all the facts laid out in the opening paragraphs are elaborated upon in the body of the release, and be sure to link your exposition of the facts to your close with a transitional paragraph or two stating or restating the theme indicated in the lead. A quote, anecdote, short phrase, or reprise of the lead usually makes for a strong close. Remember, the end is more than a summary; it's the clincher.

Here's an example of how a feature release is put together:

> *Lead:* We all expect more out of life. And some of us are lucky enough to get it. Much more.

> *Transition:* John Smith, an employee of the ABC Foundation, recently received $25,000—and that was only the beginning of much more to come. But he had already given something in return. His life.

> *Exposition:* John Smith died in Cyprus in October. . . . But not before . . .

> *Close:* John Smith never took anything from anyone. In fact, he spent all his time giving. Perhaps that's why his colleagues recently began the John Smith Foundation. As one of them said: "We didn't know what else to give him."

Formatting Releases

News and feature releases are basic tools in communicating a public relations strategy. As such, their appearance is important. To ensure that your release receives the attention it deserves, follow the formatting guidelines below:

1. Use 8½" x 11" letterhead that includes your organization's logo, name, address, and telephone number for the first

"Make sure all the facts laid out in the opening paragraphs are elaborated upon in the body of the release. . . ."

page of any release. The first page should also be slugged, or identified, as a release. If your organization doesn't have its own letterhead, type your organization's name, address, and telephone and fax numbers, single-spaced, at the top left-hand corner of an 8½" x 11" sheet of plain bond paper.

2. If you use letterhead for your releases, the name of your organization's media contact—usually the director of news operations—should be indicated, along with his or her telephone number, at the top right-hand corner of the first page. If you're using plain bond, type "CONTACT:" followed by the appropriate name and phone number at the top right-hand corner of the page.

3. If the story is for immediate release, skip two lines and type and underline "FOR IMMEDIATE RELEASE" below the media contact's name; if the story should be held for release on a particular day or at a particular time, type the exact date and/or time (e.g., "FOR RELEASE A.M., JUNE 4, 1995"); and if it doesn't really matter when the story is released, type "RELEASE AT WILL." In the case of a specific release date, make sure you get the release to its intended audience two to three days before its release date. Otherwise, editors will consider it old news and toss it in the wastebasket.

4. Leave a 1" to 1½" margin on either side of every page of the release. It can be helpful (especially in newsletter formats) to set your margins so that the copy can be lifted directly from the release and used verbatim. On an 8½" x 11" sheet of paper, setting margins at 20 (left) and 75 (right) will give you what old newspaper types call a *take*— that is, an average of 10 words a line and 25 lines a page, or about 250 words per page of copy.

5. Double-space the actual text of the release and use one side of the page only.

6. Type and center a headline and, when appropriate, a subhead about a third of the way down the first page. The headline should be boldfaced and all caps and should not run more than two lines. A subhead, if called for, should be typed in upper and lowercase letters and should be no more than two lines. Subheads should be underlined and can be be boldfaced as well.

7. Begin the first paragraph of the release with a "dateline"—for example, "NEW YORK, April 29, 1995," fol-

lowed by a space and an em dash. Make sure the dateline date is the same as the release date.

8. Indent all paragraphs four to eight spaces.

9. End each page with a complete paragraph. Do not split paragraphs or sentences between pages.

10. Center a page number at the top of every page after the first page.

11. Identify, or slug, each page after the first page in the top left-hand corner by using either the entire headline or a thematic word or phrase from the main head.

12. Finally, type "MORE" at the bottom of each page, except for the final page, which should end with "30" (the traditional Morse Code signoff), # # #, or -END-.

WORKING WITH THE MEDIA

What happens after you've carefully crafted your publicity materials and decided who should receive them? Do you call first? Or do you just send the materials? Or do you send the materials and then call? Usually, it depends on the story. Pitch calls and/or letters often are used to pique an editor's interest in a particular story. Other times, broad-based mailings with selected follow-up are almost as effective and require fewer organizational resources. You may even combine the two approaches on occasion. Here's how to pitch a story—on the phone and in writing—and how to organize a broad-based mailing.

Making a Pitch Call

There was a certain public relations person who had a telephone manner that used to be the envy of her department. On occasion, a colleague would call out, "Beth is going to make a pitch call," and half the younger account executives would crowd into her small cubicle to hear the master at work. Most of the time the calls were "cold." That is, she had a story she wanted to pitch to an editor or reporter, but she didn't know the reporter or the publication. She did have two things going for her, however: a winning phone manner and a story she had convinced herself was not only worth telling, but, more important, was worth hearing. Here's how the ensuing conversation would sound:

Beth: Hello, Mr. Smith? This is Beth C___. Did I catch you at a bad time?

Editor: No.

Beth: I'm glad. You know, it's been a crazy day for us here at [name of organization]. We've just come out with a study on the economic possibilities of redevelopment in a depressed area of [name of city]. And the phones haven't stopped ringing.

Editor: Really? What kind of things have you discovered?

Beth: I know you must be very busy, and I don't want to keep you too long, but probably the most important thing about our report is that it concludes—and I was really surprised by this myself—that for all the bad press it's received, there's probably greater potential for development in [name of the area] than in any other place like it in the Northeast.

Editor: That sounds pretty interesting.

Beth: Well, the study was commissioned by [name of reputable group], and it really contains some well-documented research as well as some interesting suggestions about what can be done in an area we once thought was beyond hope.

Editor: Is there anything you can send me?

Beth: I'd be happy to send or fax along an executive summary of the report. And if you'd like I'll call in a few days to arrange a meeting with you and our executive director to discuss the findings and what they might mean.

Editor: That sounds fine. Just fax it to me at _____.

Beth: Thanks for your time, Mr. Smith. I'll call you in a few days to set up a meeting. When would be a good time to call?

Editor: Tuesday at three.

Beth: Great. I'll talk to you then. And thanks again for your interest.

Beth had done it again. In a matter of minutes she had presented her case, personalized it, and developed a relationship with a heretofore unknown editor.

Pitch calls, like any other tool in a public relations professional's kit, are meant to spread the word about newsworthy items. Still, the most important thing to remember about a pitch call is that it should be brief and to the point. Here are some other tips for crafting an effective pitch:

- Try to establish a personal rapport with the editor or reporter on the other end of the line, even if it's a cold pitch and you've never spoken to that person before. Remember, you'll probably want to speak to him or her again.

- Get to the point—and make it interesting. As with a good news or feature story, your "lead" should be dramatic and informative enough to get the other person's attention while conveying your basic message. Instead of opening with a rambling sentence, start off with two or three short, concise sentences. Remember, editors are busy people; once you get one on the phone, you don't have much time to make your sale.

- Be ready to send the information you have to offer by mail, fax, or via a quickly arranged interview.

- Be prepared to back up your lead with relevant information—whether it's mention of a report or recent study, statistical information, or a credible statement from a well-known source.

- Be specific about the kinds of materials available for follow-up as well as about when a meeting or interview with a spokesperson can be arranged. Similarly, try to pin down your next contact with the person on the other end of the line. Don't leave it up to him or her to get back to you.

- Keep the conversation short, unless the editor wants to keep it going. The point of a pitch call is to pave the way for the next call and the one after that; in other words, to create a continuing relationship.

". . . the most important thing to remember about a pitch call is that it should be brief and to the point."

Writing a Pitch Letter

Letters We Never Finished Reading

"Dear Ms. L_____:

Tired of the Riviera, Monaco or Palm Springs? Dying to see something new and unusual? Well, I've got just the thing— Mud Island!"

—*Letter from a public relations firm, reprinted in* The New Yorker

Like a news release, a pitch letter is designed to suggest story or programming possibilities and/or to encourage coverage of an event.

While some people, particularly in the nonprofit sector, might be uncomfortable with the concept, a pitch is akin to a direct sale. The purpose of a pitch is to capture the interest of an editor or news director so that he or she will pursue a story that is close to your organization's heart. (See pages 84 and 85 for examples.)

Remember, you're not selling snake oil, you're offering valid journalistic ideas. If they're not valid, don't bother. You're wasting everyone's time, and what's worse, you're setting yourself up as an unreliable source. Some stories are stronger and more deserving of coverage than others. Other stories should only be pitched to those members of the media with whom you have a particularly good relationship. And some stories simply should not be pitched. In the final analysis, you have to choose. Be discriminating.

Once you've decided to send a pitch letter, you then have to make sure it's personalized. Although the same basic letter may be used to contact different reporters and editors at different newspapers and media outlets, it's in your best interest to make sure each one is tailored for an audience of one.

The pitch letter, like a feature release, should open with a strong lead that piques the reader's interest. A striking fact, a startling statistic, or a controversial statement are time-honored opening gambits. The letter should then jump straight into the story you want to convey. It should suggest several story angles and indicate why the story would be of interest to that editor's readers or audience. If you think it would be appropriate for a feature, make it clear that you're offering ideas for a feature. If your letter is not intended to generate a story, be specific about what kind of response you hope to generate.

Often, pitch letters are used to follow up phone conversations. In the process of tracking down the person who should receive your letter, you

"The pitch letter . . . should open with a strong lead that piques the reader's interest."

may even end up on the phone with that person. When that happens, tell the person you have a story that may be of interest to them. If that person then asks you to make your pitch over the phone, do it quickly and in as interesting a fashion as possible. Follow up your conversation with a letter that includes an introductory sentence referring to your phone conversation.

Exploratory Media Meetings

A pitch letter can also be used to request an exploratory, face-to-face meeting between a reporter and the head of your organization. Such "getting-to-know-you" meetings are designed to help set the stage for future media coverage and should achieve the following:

- establish a range of topics that the head of your organization feels comfortable discussing
- underscore your organization's expertise and give reporters an "insider's" view of it
- offer reporters suggestions as to current and future trends that might warrant coverage
- impress upon reporters the willingness of your organization to share information
- create name recognition and goodwill for the future

Broad-based Mailings and Other Distribution Strategies

For broad-based media mailings, it may not be practical—or necessary—to phone each of your contacts first. Even pitch letters are sometimes superfluous. The truth is, hard news can land without advance notice. Thus, the important questions to ask yourself are, Is my story newsworthy enough? And, Have I targeted the right people?

Each release or media mailing should be based on a separate media list, prepared just for that mailing. Though it's certainly possible to distribute a release to every major daily and weekly newspaper around the country, you should carefully consider the costs and benefits of such a strategy. If the release publicizes a story of real national interest, blanketing the country with releases might indeed get you the coverage you desire. It might also simply result in a lot of people throwing away your materials unopened.

Even if yours is a nationally relevant hard news story, you should consider limiting your mailing to the major newspapers and television

"Each release or media mailing should be based on a separate media list, prepared just for that mailing."

M Booth & Associates, Inc.

May 11, 1994

Ms. Nichole Bernier
Conde Nast Traveler
360 Madison Avenue
New York, NY 10017

Dear Ms. Bernier:

Your readers will want to bring home many souvenirs of their travels abroad this summer
-- but hepatitis isn't one of them.

While hepatitis is not a major health threat in the United States, the various types of the
disease are pandemic throughout much of the world. Hepatitis B is one of the most
common and widespread infectious diseases on the planet -- there may be as many as
300 million carriers worldwide. Hepatitis A and C are widespread in Asian countries as
well as in all of the developing world. Hepatitis E is common in Asia, Mexico and Africa.

With thousands of American travelers going abroad this summer, your readers need to
know how to protect themselves from this dangerous -- and potentially deadly -- disease.
In fact, a recent hepatitis awareness survey conducted by the New York Blood Center
found that most people don't know much about hepatitis, especially the differences
between the various forms of the disease and how they are transmitted. This lack of
knowledge can leave travelers unprotected from a serious health threat.

There are steps that travelers can take to protect themselves from hepatitis or to minimize
their risk of infection while abroad. With the summer travel season ahead, the New York
Blood Center has prepared the enclosed "Hepatitis Survival Guide" for you to share with
your readers.

If you would like additional information or would like to speak with the Blood Center's Dr.
Alfred Prince, one of the country's leading experts on the disease, about how travelers
can protect themselves, please feel free to call me at (212) 481-7000.

Sincerely,

Patricia Miller

M BOOTH & ASSOCIATES, INC.

May 3, 1994

Dear Mr. Vaughn:

Forty-something and forgetful? The bad news is that it may not all be in your mind. New findings from the Dana Consortium on Memory Loss and Aging suggest that our memories start to falter while we are in our 30s, and get worse after 40.

Barry Gordon, M.D., Ph.D., Director of the Cognitive Neurology/Neuropsychology Clinic at The Johns Hopkins Hospital in Baltimore, says that the consortium scientists still have yet to determine whether such mid-life forgetfulness is a precursor to Alzheimer's Disease or the result of modern-day "information overload" -- what happens when we expect our brains to remember too much at once, but they do know that so-called "brain exercises" -- including crossword puzzles, reading, and other activities that keep the mind active, may help us retain our memories for life.

A leading neurologist at Johns Hopkins, Dr. Gordon is a skillful and knowledgeable speaker with a depth of experience in dealing with the "aging" brain.

As you may be considering an article memory loss and aging, you may want to consider talking with Dr. Gordon and other members of the consortium on the newest findings in memory loss and aging at the Cognitive Neurology Clinic at Johns Hopkins. Dr. Gordon and his Consortium colleagues are available to discuss these new findings on memory loss and have solid advice on how men and women can maintain their memories as they age.

I've attached background on the Dana Consortium; if you are interested in pursuing this story for Prevention, please call. I can assist you in obtaining and scheduling interviews with the nation's leading neuroscientists and memory loss experts. I look forward to hearing from you.

Sincerely,

P.S. The Dana Consortium on Memory Loss and Aging is a grouping of five prestigious research centers devoted to the study of "normal" memory loss (i.e., non- disease related) and possible preventions. It is funded by the Charles A. Dana Foundation.

and radio stations in ten target regions around the country. By adopting such a strategy, you can pitch the story beforehand to those outlets, and, depending on the resources available to you, even offer a spokesperson from your organization for interviews.

In some cases, you may want to create an incentive for coverage by offering an *exclusive*—that is, a promise to a media outlet that it will have the opportunity to run the story first. Many publicists use a sophisticated technique involving "A" and "B" mailings, in which two releases with slightly different angles are offered as exclusives to two different outlets in the same city.

Once you have created your media lists and put them into some sort of database, you need to consider how best to distribute your materials. There are companies that handle this task for a fee. Among the better-known are PR Newswire, which puts releases on the wire as well as online (on the World Wide Web at http://www.prnewswire.com/), and MediaLink (on the Web at http://206.65.84.27/), which distributes video news releases via satellite and videotape. Media Distribution Service, with offices in major cities around the the country, and PIMS, Inc., with offices in New York, Los Angeles, Washington, D.C., Chicago, and London, offer set media lists to their clients, who simply check off the names of the reporters and broadcasters they'd like materials sent to and are billed accordingly.

Another increasingly popular option is broadcast fax, which involves sending a single document to multiple recipients via fax machine. The service makes sense when you are trying to reach smaller, targeted audiences, and, increasingly, it's being offered by the major media distribution companies.

Not to be overlooked are the U.S. Postal Service and overnight mail services. And there are always local messenger services, which can get a press release across town within a matter of hours.

After you've reviewed the options, determine the best distribution mix for your story and budget. You may have information or materials that simply must be sent by overnight air express; less timely information, on the other hand, can go via the regular mail. Similarly, you might want to messenger your materials to editors at key dailies and wire services for quicker action and use regular mail to send things to editors at the weeklies, where deadlines are longer.

Consult with the U.S. Postal Service about rates and delivery time for different classes of mail. Nonprofits are eligible for reduced rates from the Postal Service, but the money you save may be canceled out by the slower delivery schedules. Remember, good publicity means efficient delivery of timely communications. It may be worth spending a little more on first-class mail or messengers to do just that. Conversely, when you're faced with a tight deadline, faxing your materials may be the best approach. Be selective and creative in your choice of distribution methods.

Once your materials have been sent, don't simply call reporters or editors to see if they arrived. Editors and reporters are busy people. The last thing they need or want is a barrage of news releases of little interest or phone calls that waste time. When you call, make sure you have something to say. Provide additional information, give them an update, or describe a related event you'd like them to attend. And when an editor or reporter does use your materials, don't forget to send a thank-you note.

Faxing Etiquette

The best way to get time-sensitive information to the media is via fac-simile transmission. There are certain considerations you should keep in mind, however:

- *Decide whether the information is suitable for faxing.* Fax machines are an excellent way to inform an editor or reporter of late-breaking news. But only urgent information should be sent via fax. News organizations receive hundreds of faxes every day, and tying up a fax machine with non-pressing news stories is a good way to get on the bad side of any reporter or editor. If time allows—and you should do everything in your power to make sure it does—mailing news releases is still the best way to get your information to the appropriate parties.

  The length of the release is another consideration. If it's more than 15 pages, don't fax it; instead, send it via messenger or overnight mail.

- *Alert the editor/reporter to the imminent arrival of your materials.* Not all reporters and editors like to receive faxes, and many news desks will request that the information be sent by mail. However, if the reporter/editor is informed of the news release beforehand, and especially if it's late-breaking news, they'll usually be more than happy to supply you with a fax number. This can work to your advantage, since in many instances a reporter/editor will give you the number to his or her own fax machine instead of the number listed in media directories.

- *Never assume.* Never assume that your materials were received, even if your machine confirms that the fax went through. Because news organizations receive faxes by the hundreds, the chances are good that any single

". . . tying up a fax machine with non-pressing news stories is a good way to get on the bad side of any reporter or editor."

"Editors and reporters are busy people; they don't have time to sort through unimportant or trivial information."

PUBLICITY DOs AND DON'Ts

The give-and-take of direct contact is the basis of most day-to-day publicity work. Therefore, some basic *dos* and *don't*s are in order.

1. Never mislead a reporter knowingly. Good reporters can detect puffery or an outright lie before it's left your mouth. And once you're caught, your credibility is destroyed.

2. Make sure your story is newsworthy. Editors and reporters are busy people; they don't have time to sort through unimportant or trivial information. What they do appreciate is a solid, factual, clearly outlined story.

3. If you don't know the answer to a question, say so. You can always find the answer and call back.

4. If there's a reason you can't answer a question, say so. A good reporter will respect your honesty.

5. Never use pressure to get publicity or favorable coverage. Your contact may be doing you a favor, but his or her staff could feel put upon, and they will remember.

6. Do not overwrite or overthink your news story. Keep news releases as short as possible.

7. Check and double-check all information distributed to the media. Accuracy is essential.

8. Use the phone wisely. A telephone call following up a release is important. It can tell you that your release arrived and it gives you a chance to speak personally with the reporter or editor to whom it was sent.

9. Stay off editors' backs. If your story has merit, it will run; if it doesn't, it won't.

10. If you give information to an editor over the phone, follow up the conversation immediately in writing. Always include your name, address,

telephone number, and fax number (if you have one).

11. Keep your promises—all of them—or don't make them. If you promise to call a reporter back with additional information, make sure you do. If you promise to gather additional information, make sure you do it in a timely fashion.

12. Send your news releases and media advisories by first-class mail or fax to a specific person or title. An advance release should arrive at least two days prior to the event it publicizes.

13. Don't call top editors, publishers, and broadcasters with anything less than a big story. If you don't know the name of the person to whom you should send a release, a simple call to the station or newspaper will get you that information.

14. If you contact more than one editor at the same media outlet with the same story, let them all know what you've done. List somewhere on your materials the names of all the editors receiving that release.

15. Keep in touch. The point of making media contacts is to serve them. Do everything in your power to establish yourself as a valued information source.

16. Do your homework. Tailor your materials to fit the medium. Familiarize yourself with media deadlines and the ground rules for submitting copy and photographs, then observe them.

17. Let one person be the media contact for your organization.

18. Don't organize a news conference unless you have something of regional, national, or international import to share.

19. Keep abreast of the reporters and reporting in your field, and pay special attention to story angles that haven't yet been covered.

fax may be misplaced and never reach its destination. To be safe, contact the editor/reporter within an hour of faxing the release to confirm that it was received.

SPECIAL PRINT PUBLICITY TECHNIQUES AND STRATEGIES

Newspaper Editorials

There's no secret to or magic involved in securing editorial support for your cause or organization. Instead, it requires the same common sense and hard work that you put into your other media relations activities. The aim of your efforts should be something more than a story, however. Your goal should be a statement by the news organization that says, in effect, that the issue your group is addressing is a vital one deserving of public attention and support.

"Editorial support can go a long way toward advancing a nonprofit organization's agenda."

Editorial support can go a long way toward advancing a nonprofit organization's agenda. It can help an organization achieve its stated goals by publicizing a particular action, or help to rally support in the community for the organization, whether during a fund drive or in the face of pointed attacks.

Of course, there are a variety of ways to attract the editorial support of news organizations. The most obvious is to arrange a meeting with a representative of an editorial board.

Meetings with Editorial Boards. Although it may sound imposing, a meeting with an editorial writer or editorial board need not be intimidating. Before you arrange such a meeting, however, it's a good idea to have already generated some media attention, either by having spoken out about a particular issue of community or national importance, by having been the point organization in a well-publicized action, or through your own publicity materials.

Meetings between editorial writers or boards and groups seeking support for their cause are not unusual. In fact, they are a necessary aspect of the day-to-day work of editors, editorial writers, broadcasters, and publishers. The various news media know full well that the only way to fairly cover an issue or an organization is armed with an understanding of that issue or organization.

To arrange a meeting with an editorial board, write the editorial page editor, the publisher's office, or the executive editor's office. State your purpose and why you feel a meeting at this time is a good idea. For example, you might:

- be seeking support for a particular issue or action;
- feel that certain statements picked up by the media were misleading and need to be clarified;
- want to draw attention to the start of a major fund drive, which, if successful, will mean a lot to your community;
- be celebrating an organizational anniversary and feel that it's a good opportunity to remind people about your organization's importance to the community, as well as to tell them what you hope to accomplish in the years ahead.

This kind of self-promotion may sound a bit presumptuous, but keep in mind that you are dealing with people whose work revolves around opinion and subjective statements and beliefs. Be bold and wear your passion for an issue or cause on your sleeve; more often than not, you'll be respected for it.

At the same time, don't forget about the details. Once a meeting has been agreed to, don't waste any time letting the other party know who will represent your group at the meeting and be sure to provide his or her background. Don't crowd the session with your own people. If you really want to present a focused picture of your cause or issue and provide consistent answers to the questions asked, a single spokesperson is best.

Be sure, as well, to prepare a variety of materials as *leave-behinds.* Thank-you letters are also in order. If an organizational spokesperson attends the meeting alone, debrief him or her as soon as possible in order to determine the next step. And if follow-up with the editors or reporters who cover your beat is needed, be sure to provide the appropriate materials or answers in a timely fashion.

"Letters to the Editor"

One way to express your organization's views or to counter misleading editorials or news reports is through the "Letters to the Editor" section. A letter to the editor can be used to raise a point about an issue in the news, oppose or support the actions of an official agency, direct attention to a problem, or gain a little publicity for your organization and its programs. Letters to the editor can also be an effective and ongoing means of communicating your organization's views to a wider audience.

A letter to the editor is always sent to the editor of the editorial page and should be neatly typed in standard letter format, with the salutation "To the Editor" at the top of the page. The tie-in with a particular news item or editorial should be handled in the opening sentence. (When

"If you really want to present a focused picture of your cause or issue and provide consistent answers to the questions asked, a single spokesperson is best."

responding to a newspaper editorial or article, refer to the piece in question by date and title.) The body of the letter should be brief and focused, and should supply any details you feel were missing from the earlier coverage of your organization. The person who signs the letter on behalf of your organization should be identified by name and position. (See below for an example.)

Be sure to follow the guidelines (e.g., maximum number of words) of the periodical or publication to which you're sending the letter. The publication has the right to edit your letter, but an editor will probably check with you first. An editor also will usually check to make sure you actually wrote the letter and that someone did not falsely use your name or the name of your organization.

Notification policies vary from paper to paper and publication to publication. It doesn't hurt to ask, but don't expect an answer, even if you agree with the position staked out by a publication or laud a paper's editorial position. Remember, just by sending the letter, you're communicating your organization's message.

In addition to those already mentioned, there are several other ways in which your organization can use the "Letters to the Editor" section.

Too-Early Pregnancy

To the Editor:

The image of single, teen-age parents raising children kept recurring in our series of articles on violent children (May 15-18). However, in discussing possible solutions, you neglected prevention of teenage pregnancy, despite the existence of effective initiatives to fight this problem.

Here at Inwood house, we tackle the issue of teen-age pregnancy daily by helping young people take control of their reproductive choices, yet we see the issue largely ignored by the mainstream media.

The problems of poverty, lack of opportunity, family disintegration and the violence engendered are complicated, requiring multiple solutions.

Helping young people avoid too-early parenthood must be high on the list of priorities if we are to reverse the frightening trends your articles portray.   JOY FALLEK
Director, Teen-Age Choice Program
Inwood House
New York, May 20, 1994

1. Have various members of your board write letters to the editor, with each board member addressing a single point (or two) in concise fashion (a paragraph or three). If the board member has a particular expertise or outside affiliation that's relevant to the point raised in his or her letter, make sure it's mentioned in the body of the letter.

2. Ask high-profile friends of your organization—the higher the profile, the better—to write letters in support of the organization and its programs.

3. If you still don't feel your message is getting across, ask for an editorial board meeting to further explain your position. At the least, ask to meet with the reporter who wrote the piece you think is misleading or uninformed. Most reporters are willing to be educated. And you may be educated in turn.

Op-Ed Articles

When *The New York Times* began running a page of comment from readers opposite their editorial page, the op-ed was born. Other newspapers, from *The Wall Street Journal* to *The Washington Post*, soon followed suit. So did news magazines such as *Newsweek* and *Time*.

With hard work and a little luck, you too can have an op-ed piece published. Your first step should be to obtain length specifications from the op-ed page editor; 800 words is usually the maximum. Next, write the piece. As its name implies, an op-ed piece should be timely and have a definite point of view. It should also be clear, focused, and well-written. Get someone whose judgment and "ear" you respect to read it, and make revisions as necessary. (See page 94 for an example.)

Even then, there's no assurance your piece will be published. But if you write the right piece at the right time and direct it to the right publication, you just might get your turn. And even if your piece isn't published, there are other ways you can use it—in brochure copy, as a direct-mail piece to supporters and public officials, or in paid advertisements.

Bylined Articles

Trade publications and community newspapers often accept articles and columns written by outside parties. To pursue this option, first become familiar with the targeted outlet and then contact its editor or publisher with a particular story idea. For example, if your organization is involved

". . . an op-ed piece should be timely and have a definite point of view."

Building Refuge And Hope Inside Rwanda

By Mary Moran

AS I prepare to leave for a new assignment – as a nurse for the International Rescue Committee in Goma, Zaire – I know what I will tell the Rwandan refugees: "Go home. Go quickly. There are good things happening there and returning is the best hope for you and your family."

One month ago I traveled inside Rwanda on a mission for the US-based Women's Commission for Refugee Women and Children. I met with dozens of women working to rebuild their country. I traveled in rebel-held territory because the only escort available to me was through the Rwandan Patriotic Front (RPF). Mine was a humanitarian mission, to determine what was happening to the women and children.

I found a surprising thing: Although terrible destruction and death were everywhere, there were also signs of hope.

Before international help arrived, the RPF had methodically searched the countryside and had rescued people hiding in the marshes, the fields, and the hills where they had fled from the militia's deadly rampage. The RPF took survivors to the towns that the rebels had won. Schools, churches, and vacated homes were converted into shelters for thousands of displaced persons. Some were even able to return to their own homes.

Women are playing an important role in this effort. The Women's Organization of the RPF was placing orphaned and abandoned children with families or in orphanages. Rwandan women lawyers, nurses, teachers, and other professionals helped coordinate their activities with those of the international relief agencies. Since 1990 the women's group has been working with women throughout Rwanda, promoting health, education, and income-generating projects.

When the war broke out in April, members of the women's group devoted their energies to crisis intervention and humanitarian assistance. They called upon the international community to help them. When I visited, they were working in conjunction with international agencies to place abandoned children and orphans with families, to set up hospitals, and to bury the dead.

Most important, the RPF refused to discuss ethnicity and provided humanitarian assistance to anyone who needed help. When whether there were difficulties between the Hutus and Tutsis in these areas, the women told me, "Please do not ask about this. We discourage this form of thinking in order to begin the healing process of our people."

In the town of Rutare, 105,000 displaced people sought shelter in June. International relief organizations provided health care, food, shelter, and sanitation serv-

> **The women told me, 'Please do not ask about [Hutu-Tutsi conflicts]. We discourage this form of thinking in order to begin the healing process.'**

ices. The RPF coordinated activities and provided security. I saw this humanitarian activity taking place in much of the rebel-held territory.

The United States and the international community must build on these efforts in order to persuade the refugees to return home. Although international assistance is critical to the life-saving operations on the borders, the majority of funds must be devoted to programs inside Rwanda that will improve people's lives in a lasting way. Roads must be repaired, houses rebuilt, and most important, families reunited. The Women's Organization of the RPF and other women's groups have much to offer and should be included in all relief and development projects.

One of the first steps for the international community is to end the current crisis by shutting down Radio Mille Collines, the propaganda station of the former government of Rwanda, which exhorted people to leave their homes and villages. While I was in Rwanda last month, Radio Mille Collines was inciting thousands to slaughter their Tutsi neighbors, saying the Tutsis were evil.

For the past two weeks these radio broadcasts have convinced the population that the RPF is set on revenge and will murder and torture all Hutus. This misinformation must be countered with radio broadcasts from credible sources, such as the United Nations, providing news about what is really happening inside Rwanda. The refugees should know the truth – that there is no fighting inside Rwanda or revenge-killing by the RPF.

When I arrive in Zaire, I will work day and night to care for the sick and dying. But I am convinced that the only hope for the refugees is for them to return home.

The US and the international community can help by providing the funds, logistical assistance, and security needed by the people of Rwanda so that – together with international relief agencies – they can rebuild their country.

■ *Mary Moran is a professional nurse on a short-term assignment for the International Rescue Committee in Zaire. She wrote this article before leaving for the refugee camps earlier this week.*

RWANDAN REFUGEES AT A CAMP IN ZAIRE, JULY 1994/ JACK DABAGHIAN – REUTERS

in early childhood education, you might propose an article in a trade publication such as *Education Week* about the future of such programs in light of municipal, state, and federal budget cutting. If your organization is working to increase neighborhood participation in recycling, an article about the cost savings of such a program might be of interest to your local community newspaper.

Newspaper Interviews: How to Answer Questions

> *"Many executives still view the media as an extension of the public relations apparatus. That is, let 'em tell the world how great we are, but it's none of their business when things aren't so hot."*
> —Jack Bernstein, "Why P.R. Gets Flak,"
> *The New York Times*

It's time to meet the press. How can you ensure that your organization is viewed as a respected source for a story?

For starters, have all initial press queries directed to one central source—either the executive director or the public relations office. This will go a long way toward keeping the stories generated by your organization consistent and clear. Although the policy will vary from organization to organization, in general only specified members of the public relations office should speak for the organization as a whole. Once you've settled on the best policy for your organization, stick to it.

Second, assume that all statements made will be on the record. Avoid giving out information and following it with, "Of course, that's off the record." While you don't always have to have your name attached to a particular comment or piece of information as the source, at the very least you should allow it to be used and attributed to "an official but anonymous source."

Try to cooperate with the media at all times, even if a story has the potential to cast your organization in a less-than-flattering light. Just be careful about what you say. And unless a reporter objects, in potentially damaging situations try to have a public relations officer from your organization present.

Third, state the facts and don't editorialize. Review any scripted statements you plan to make and try to anticipate questions to which you may not have the answers. The last thing you want to do is to make the reporter's life more difficult or create hostility toward your organization by saying, "Find out for yourself." If the facts are out in the open, be open about them. Similarly, if your organization has put out a misleading or incorrect statement, don't be afraid to correct it. And if you really

"Try to cooperate with the media at all times, even if a story has the potential to cast your organization in a less-than-flattering light."

"It's always better to say you didn't know or were wrong than to read just how wrong you were the next day."

don't feel comfortable answering a question, don't. It's always better to say you didn't know or were wrong than to read just how wrong you were the next day.

GENERATING PUBLICITY ON TELEVISION AND RADIO

In addition to the steady stream of pitch calls, letters, and releases to the print media, a special effort should be made to garner exposure on radio and television. Try to "sell" local TV stations on the idea of taping a story about your organization, and make an effort to get spokespersons from your organization on radio and TV talk shows and news programs.

Once upon a time, the only way you could reach a television audience in a variety of media markets was through a media tour, with your spokesperson traveling from city to city for individual on-air interviews. Today, with advances in technology, a satellite media tour in which your spokesperson sits in a studio and is interviewed via satellite by stations across the country is the way to go.

Working with TV and Radio

Get to know the electronic media. Familiarize yourself with news-oriented and public-affairs programming in your market. Credits at the end of programs, radio and television listings in your local paper, and media directories are among the sources you can use to keep up-to-date on which programs are looking for what types of guests. Some of these sources also provide the names of contacts who can answer your questions about getting on the air. Most television and radio news shows have assignment desks that decide which stories they will cover. In the case of interview programs, the producer or talent coordinator usually books the guests.

To a surprising degree, members of the broadcast media (more so than members of the print media) are willing to accept phone calls without first having received an introductory letter. But before you pick up the phone, be sure you're familiar with the show's audience and format. At the risk of stating the obvious, nationally broadcast shows look for nationally known celebrities and topics with national implications, while local shows are more apt to take local guests and are usually enthusiastic about out-of-town visitors. In most cases, the station is the best source for audience demographic information and actual ratings numbers.

When you call a radio or television station, try to emulate "Beth's" phone style (see pages 80–81). The first thing you should do is ask the person on the other end of the line whether it's a good time to talk.

Generally, calling right before or right after a show's scheduled time slot should be avoided. If the person you've reached is willing to talk, be prepared to quickly mention your spokesperson and the topic you feel is worthy of discussion, as well as two or three reasons why the topic is timely and your spokesperson is the best person to talk about it.

Often, a newspaper article that features your organization or spokesperson, or one that touches on a topic your spokesperson is qualified to discuss, can be parlayed into airtime. It's your job to make the contact person aware of such print media coverage. Just as often, however, a call must be followed up with a pitch letter and background material. If that's what is required, be sure to follow up immediately, since radio and television people are continually besieged by calls and requests for on-air time. (See pages 98–99 for an example.)

On rare occasions, members of the broadcast media may contact your organization about an appearance. In such instances, it's your job to decide whether radio or television exposure is in your organization's best interest, as opposed to that of the radio or television show's. Don't allow yourself to be persuaded by the "sex appeal" of such exposure. Consider your short- and long-range communications objectives and try to determine whether they will be served by the opportunity at hand.

If the producer of a particular radio or television program expresses interest in having a spokesperson from your organization appear, be sure to ask whether the appearance will be an exclusive in that city, and if so, during what time period. Though usually not the case with regularly scheduled news programs, sometimes a producer will insist that a spokesperson or personality not appear on another channel in that city for a specific period of time preceding his or her appearance on the program in question.

If you decide to let your spokesperson appear and have agreed on a date, confirm the arrangement in writing, making sure to include the date, place, proposed topic, person or persons to attend, and the time your spokesperson will arrive at the studio (for makeup, etc.). In the world of print, things can be rescheduled when there's a mix-up and the world doesn't come to an end. Not so in radio and television, where, if you're scheduled to appear and for some reason you don't show, it can be disastrous.

Once your spokesperson is booked, it's time to "press the press." In other words, try to get a listing, photo, highlight, or even a column mention on the TV or radio pages of newspapers in your area featuring the fact that your organization's spokesperson will be on such and such a show to discuss such and such a topic.

"Consider your short- and long-range communications objectives and try to determine whether they will be served by the opportunity at hand."

M BOOTH & ASSOCIATES, INC.

July 22, 1994

<u>By Facsimile</u>
Bob Epstein
Senior Producer
CBS Weekend News/Sunday News
524 West 57th Street
New York, NY 10019

Dear Mr. Epstein:

Right now, this country's top science and math teachers are revving up for a ride on the Infobahn -- and their students will be going along for the ride. As of May 1994, approximately 35,000 students in over 1,000 classrooms (including 22 countries across the globe) were linked up on the Internet via AT&T's Learning Network. They will soon be joined by the teachers in this summer's AT&T Teachers and Technology Institute.

From now until July 28, 48 middle school and high school educators -- chosen by the Governors of their home states -- will be travelling through the research corridors of Bell Labs out onto the information highway, via networked "learning circles" that are transforming the classrooms of the '90s. Attached is background on how the Learning Network got started and who is participating.

The next two weeks offer some great opportunities to see what's going on in this "summer camp for teachers." Here are a few examples:

•   **Monday, July 25, 9:30 a.m., Crawford Hill, Holmdel, New Jersey**

Nobel Prize-winning physicist Arno Penzias will join the teachers on a hilltop in New Jersey, for a look at the giant radio antenna that helped him formulate the "big bang" theory of the origin of the universe. This is an on-site visit, not a lecture, and there will be interaction between Penzias and the teachers. (The B-roll includes footage of Penzias from last year that gives you an idea of his dynamic and energetic personality -- he really motivates the teachers.)

470 Park Avenue South New York, New York 10016 (212) 481-7000 fax 212 481-9440

July 22, 1994
Page 2

- **Monday, July 25, 11:00 a.m. - 1:00 p.m. and 2:00 - 4:00 p.m. -- Bell Labs, Holmdel, New Jersey**

  Teachers will break up into smaller groups for a look at what's going in this state-of-the-art research facility. Brilliant lasers, fiber-optic cables, and other cutting-edge communications technologies will be demonstrated. (See B-roll for a short clip of last year's tour.)

- **Wednesday, July 27, 10:00 a.m. - noon, Global Communications Briefing Center, Basking Ridge New Jersey**

  The future edges closer with a demonstration of the Telemedia Distance Learning Link system. This is a program that allows students across the country to participate in a visually-linked interactive classroom setting (you may have seen this on the "You Will" ads).

- **Thursday, July 28, 1:00 - 3:00 p.m., Network Operations Center, Bedminster, New Jersey**

  A trip into the heart of one of the biggest communications systems in the country, where a wall of over 75 monitors tracks millions of calls a minute.

Given the short notice, dates and times can be re-arranged for later in the week if necessary. On any given day throughout the Institute, there will be opportunities to view the teachers working in teams on project ideas, trying out new technologies and getting acquainted with the Learning Network via communications with the 1993 mentors.

I hope this information helps bring alive some of the stories contained in the events of the next two weeks -- and beyond. I'll be in touch to get your reactions.

Sincerely,

Emily Whitfield

Attachments

Editorials on Radio and Television

Many television and radio stations set aside time to do a little editorializing. The best way to find out which stations in your area do so is to call and ask.

The procedure for getting your organization or programs mentioned in a television or radio editorial is much the same as with a newspaper. Write to the editorial director, enclose the necessary background materials, and request the station's editorial support.

The same procedure applies when you feel it's necessary to go on record in opposition to an editorial position taken by an electronic media outlet. Once an editorial has been broadcast, the station, under FCC regulations, will solicit comments or opposing viewpoints from what the FCC calls "responsible bodies." Although unaffiliated individuals can respond to these calls, it's more common for spokespersons representing organized segments of the community to be given airtime. If a spokesperson from your organization is invited to appear on camera, he or she will be told how much time they have—usually 30 to 60 seconds, or two to three paragraphs. That's roughly 60 to 120 words, so make sure they all count.

When preparing an on-air rebuttal, the rules of good writing apply:

- Limit the number of ideas you plan to address.

- Write and then rewrite your materials.

- State your position clearly and succinctly. If, for example, WXYZ-TV advocates the close of all day-care facilities in a particular community because it believes them to be poorly managed, refer to your disagreement with that opinion in your opening paragraph: "A recent WXYZ-TV editorial noting mismanagement in our community's day-care facilities called for their closing. There are 40,000 kids in our community with mothers that need to work and who themselves need and deserve some caring attention. We think there's a better way to change management practices at community day-care facilities and still make sure those kids aren't neglected." Follow your opening with your solution to the problem in the second paragraph and use the last paragraph to summarize and clinch your organization's position.

- Avoid name-calling or innuendo, which, in extreme cases, can open you to legal action and, at the very least, can make you and your organization look foolish and petty.

Creating Visuals for Television

The most important component of television publicity is good visuals—whether tape, photographs, or 35mm slides. Television is a medium that likes action, even in a "talking heads" format. If you're attempting to interest a news program in taping a story, select a location that's visually appealing (preferably near the station), at a time of day that's convenient for station personnel (usually midmorning until 2 P.M.). If the taping is to be indoors, make sure electrical outlets are available.

Sometimes TV stations will accept tape shot by outside parties (most prefer 3/4-inch, although certain markets require Beta). If your organization has the resources to create its own taped pieces, make sure they include a *voiceover*—a second audio track comprised of explanatory narration lasting a minute to a minute and a half—and are accompanied by a script. You should also send along a *B roll* with sound bites for the station's use in editing the piece. Taped pieces should be no more than three to five minutes in length; longer pieces will be edited as the show's producer sees fit.

The simplest kind of TV visual aid is a photograph. If you intend to use a photo on TV, make sure it's a dull- or matte-finished (not glossy) print mounted on 11" x 14" cardboard—otherwise known as a *ballop card*—or a 35mm slide. You can also incorporate other types of visual aids into your presentation, including charts, graphs, and your organization's logo. All such aids should be sent to the show's producer as *stats*, black-and-white reproductions with the appropriate color swatches attached. Because visual aids are scanned into computers that digitize the images and allow producers to format them as needed, the above types of materials are preferred (though most television stations have the equipment to digitize almost any type of image). Any visual aid you send along should be accompanied by a cover letter, a script or storyboard (when appropriate), and a self-addressed, stamped postcard for the station manager to acknowledge receipt of the materials.

Making the Most of an Interview

There is a direct correlation between how well you prepare for a television or radio interview and how well you come across in the actual interview. By anticipating the kinds of questions you'll be asked and deciding on the message or messages you want to convey, you'll avoid embarrassment due to error or ignorance. If you pay attention to the following areas, you should come off as both knowledgeable and engaging.

1. *Preparation*—Preparation is the key. You're the expert on the subject, so be sure you know what you're talking about.

"By anticipating the kinds of questions you'll be asked and deciding on the message or messages you want to convey, you'll avoid embarrassment due to error or ignorance."

Rehearse answers to questions that might pose problems. Know your audience and gauge your language and answers accordingly. Avoid technical words and jargon. Find out in advance how long the interview will last so you can be sure to cover the points you want to make in the time allotted.

2. *Media training/aids*—Take a training workshop. There are firms that specialize in training executives for media interviews and speaking engagements. A typical workshop will include tips on how to present your message with enthusiasm, how to make and maintain eye contact with the audience, how to answer difficult questions, how to get the name of your organization across to the audience without seeming too "commercial," and how to speak in sound bytes. Often, these training sessions can be customized to your organization's particular needs.

3. *At the interview*—Arrive early. Get accustomed to the surroundings and try to establish a rapport with the interviewer(s). Avoid "talking off the record." Ask questions about the format of the interview instead: Will it be live or taped? Will there be other guests? Respect the interviewer's ability to do his or her job. It's your job to know the topic. It's the interviewer's job to ask questions. Relax and try to enjoy the experience. Let your enthusiasm for the topic come through.

4. *Your presentation*—Be brief and to the point. Decide in advance the message or messages you want to get across. Television and radio formats are fast-paced and tend to cover many subjects in a short period of time. As your on-air time is likely to be limited, stress the major points and avoid unnecessary or obscure details. If additional comment is needed, the interviewer will ask for it.

Start the interview with your most important message and try to establish an upbeat tone. If the interview is not covering material of value, say something like, "I think it's important that we talk about . . . ," or "You might be interested to know that . . ."

Speak the truth and stress the positive. Negative statements can make you sound defensive. Speak slowly and softly when you want to emphasize a point. Your listeners will make an extra effort to really listen. Most importantly, reference by name the thing you're promoting as often as possible. Listeners or viewers who just tuned in will want to know what you're discussing.

"Speak the truth and stress the positive. Negative statements can make you sound defensive."

5. *Interacting with the interviewer*—Listen carefully. If the interviewer strays from the topic, swing the conversation back your way by saying, "That's true, but think about this . . . ," or "That may appear to be the case, but not when you consider . . ." If the interviewer presents erroneous information as the truth, correct him, or else the audience will assume otherwise. Don't be charmed by the interviewer's personality or your own wit. Remain calm, rational, and polite at all times. Getting angry or flustered will not serve your cause.

6. *Style*—Avoid clichés. Avoid "uhms," "ahs," and phrases such as "Let me think about that." Don't patronize your interviewer. Avoid statements like "That's a good question . . . ," or "I'm glad you asked that." Use a short pause to emphasize a point, change the subject, add suspense, or allow the audience to "catch its breath."

7. *Your personal appearance*—If you're going to be interviewed on television, pay special attention to your appearance. You have to *appear* to be sincere and knowledgeable as well as sound convincing. Wear clothes that won't distract from the message you're trying to convey. If you'll be under hot studio lights for any length of time, be sure to wear lightweight clothing. If you're going to be seated during the interview, be sure to wear pants and socks that cover your ankles when your legs are crossed. Wear long-sleeved pastel-colored shirts. Avoid big, bright jewelry and loud ties. Watch for nervous tics such as tapping your feet or shaking your leg. Don't hold anything in your hands. Maintain eye contact with your interviewer. Sit up straight, but not too straight. If you relax too much you'll look sloppy; if you're too erect you'll look nervous. Don't walk away from the set or assume an off-camera manner until you're sure you are really off-camera. Practice at home.

Radio Placement

Using radio to publicize your organization and its programs is almost the same as using TV, except you don't have to worry about the visuals. Radio news assignment desks work like TV assignment desks, although television stations often have more personnel on hand to cover events. As a result, radio frequently uses news release information directly from media packets.

*"Beeper
interviews, or
actualities, are
a great way of
getting on
radio without
having to go
to the studio."*

Radio interviews, which can be conducted as part of a news or talk format, are excellent vehicles for obtaining exposure. You'll want to check lead times, however, since popular radio talk programs tend to be booked well in advance—sometimes as much as three to six weeks.

Radio News Beepers. *Radio news beepers* get their name from the sound made by a tape recorder recording over the telephone. Beeper interviews, or *actualities,* are a great way of getting on radio without having to go to the studio.

The best way to arrange a beeper interview is to call the station's news assignment desk, pitch your story, and ask the person on the other end of the line whether the station might be interested in setting up a beeper interview with a spokesperson from your organization. If they say yes, at the appointed time call the station, put your spokesperson on the phone, and wait for the beep. These kinds of interviews are especially popular with all-news programs, which often don't have the manpower to send a reporter to every newsworthy event.

Special Materials for Radio. Audio materials you might want to supply to a radio station can include musical recordings and taped interviews on cassettes or reel-to-reel. Taped interviews should include a music component and, when possible, should use a well-known personality's voice. If you can't get a celebrity, use a professional announcer.

Many radio stations accept audio material for use as public-service announcements. Any tape sent to a radio station can include several spots, or segments, although you should try to limit them to 10- , 20- , and 30-second spots, or just 30- and 60-second spots. Printed scripts can also be submitted to radio stations. They must be clear, short, and easy to read, however. Avoid complicated grammatical constructions or unusual words. Spell out numbers and spell hard-to-pronounce names phonetically. Triple-space your script and type it in capital letters. And before you send it to the station, read it aloud for clarity and pacing.

NEWS CONFERENCES

News conferences are an important tool for announcing innovative programs and explaining new ideas and complicated issues to the media.

Before you can organize a successful news conference—that is, one for which reporters show up and which results in a story a newspaper or TV station can use—there is one key question that must be answered: *Is the story newsworthy enough to justify reporters leaving their desks and traveling across town to cover it?* In this case, "newsworthy enough" means:

- the story is immediate;
- the story can compete successfully with the thousands of other breaking stories;
- the story cannot be done justice by a news release alone (e.g., the news conference amplifies the story while giving reporters an opportunity to question key participants); and, in the case of television,
- the story can be made visual.

If your story meets these criteria, a news conference is in order. Below are some guidelines to follow to help ensure its success.

1. Schedule your news conference for a Tuesday, Wednesday, or Thursday morning. Mondays and Fridays are busy days for most journalists, and weekends are non-starters, unless you have something particularly dramatic to announce. Avoid early morning or afternoon events. Anything later than 2:30 P.M. makes it difficult for TV news crews, who need to get raw footage back to the studio for editing before the early evening broadcasts. Eleven A.M. is the ideal starting time for a news conference.

2. Make sure your news conference doesn't run more than an hour. Ideally, it should last 20 to 30 minutes, with your announcement presented by one or two key spokespersons first, followed by a question-and-answer session.

3. Carefully target your invitations. Assemble two media lists: one should include the names of journalists vitally interested in the subject; the second might include the names of journalists with only a marginal interest in the subject. A media advisory containing the essential information is the best way to alert the press. (See pages 110–111 and 112–113 for examples.) For those reporters you know well, consider attaching a personal note to the advisory.

   Invitations to the media should go out no more than a week in advance of the conference. Follow-up calls to encourage attendance should be made two to three days in advance.

4. Select a site that will help present your story and which is also convenient to the media outlets you have targeted. It can be a theater, a rented space in a hotel or other facility, a "location" site, or even a conference room in your organization's headquarters. Many public relations professionals believe that by offering food and an attractive site,

"Avoid early morning or afternoon events . . . . Eleven A.M. is the ideal starting time for a news conference."

choosing a facility with a particularly good view, or inviting celebrities to the event, reporters and cameras will show up. They may be right. But it doesn't mean the media will report your story.

In selecting a site, consider the availablity of electrical outlets, platforms, telephones, and typewriters and computers. Security, audiovisual aids and equipment, and the room's size should also be considered. There should be sufficient space to accommodate TV cameras, though too large a space can end up looking empty if the turnout is light.

Depending on the nature of your story, there may be times when you'll want to reach audiences in different locations. In these cases, a satellite news conference is both a useful and dramatic approach.

PHOTOS—HOW TO MAKE NEWS WITH PICTURES

Good photographs can be excellent attention-getters and, thus, excellent publicity tools. They can be used to amplify a news or feature story, or used alone as a photo feature. Even the standard award presentation photo can be handled creatively.

When dealing with dailies and weekly newspapers, photos should be sent to the photo editor. Wire services also use photos. (Photo editors have earlier deadlines than other editors, so be sure to check in advance.) Any photos you send should be 8" x 10" black-and-white glossies with lots of contrast; a 5" x 7" print is also acceptable if it's a headshot accompanying an announcement release. Under no circumstance should smaller prints be sent.

Although most photo editors will crop photos to fit the space available, a photograph's appeal can be enhanced before you send it. A photograph stands a better chance of being used if it captures a single idea, so limit the number of people in the shot, try to include some action, and avoid run-of-the-mill group arrangements and camera angles. Do not write on the front or back of the photo. Type the caption neatly on white paper and glue or tape it to the back of the photo, so that the caption sheet can be folded up over the front of the photo.

When preparing a mass-mailing of black-and-white photos, it's usually cheaper and faster to use 8" x 10" machine-glossy prints created from an 8" x 10" copy negative. The original copy neg should have lots of contrast and be of exceptional quality to stand up to multiple printings without deterioration. Always use the original copy neg when ordering additional prints.

"A photograph stands a better chance of being used if it captures a single idea. . . ."

A copy negative costs from $9 to $13; machine prints cost about 35 to 50 cents per copy. Some publicists save money by including up to eight different shots on a single 8" x 10" print, thereby offering photo editors a choice of shots. Each shot should be easy to "read"—that is, it should have a single subject as its focus and, to the extent possible, it should be shot in close-up. Use a grease pencil to label each shot on the back of the print and include a description of the various subjects on a caption sheet. Multiple picture arrangements usually don't work for group scenes.

Color Versus Black-and-White

Today, there is an incredible demand for color photos as editors look for ways to brighten the pages of their newspapers. More and more newspapers are using run-of-paper (ROP) color on a daily basis. (Out of the 1,100 daily papers served by the AP, nearly all of them have the capability to run color.)

It is common practice for publicists to send a list of available color photos to magazines rather than the shots themselves. If you decide to send the shots themselves, 35mm color slides or larger super slides are the preferred format. Though they can be retouched, type C color prints are used less frequently.

Digital Photography

A revolution has taken place in the way newspapers handle photographs. Photos can now be stored and recalled digitally using CD-ROM technology. A recent AP study revealed that more than half its 1,100 subscribing newspapers had CD-ROM players, and it is estimated that in the next several years every major newspaper will utilize the technology. CD-ROM is a terrific way to store photographs that are likely to be used again and again (e.g., photos of high-profile executives, familiar landmarks or monuments, etc.). Photo images can also be sent electronically by services such as AP PhotoExpress, which transmits digital photographs instantaneously to newspapers around the country.

Slides and Transparencies

Thirty-five millimeter slides can be used:

- for distribution to magazines and newspapers;
- as visuals for television appearances; and

"Today, there is an incredible demand for color photos as editors look for ways to brighten the pages of their newspapers."

A NEWS CONFERENCE CHECKLIST

Day Before the Event

- Make certain that materials, including news releases, news packets, photos and captions, scripts of speeches, and audiovisual presentations, have been prepared and approved and that names are spelled correctly on IDs and name tags.

- Have a photographer lined up in the event no wire photographer shows. Or have a photographer from your own organization on standby as a backup for reporters who do not bring their own photographer.

- Get a complete list of reporters who plan to attend. Telephone those who have not responded to your invitation, as well as those who have responded affirmatively. Remind them of the time and location of the event and why they should come. Offer transportation to those who may need it. If a reporter cannot attend but still seems interested in the event, either arrange an interview with the principals following the conference, or messenger over a media packet and related materials (including photos, if requested) on the day of the event.

- Go to the site of the event. Set up any displays you may have, run through any audiovisual materials that will be used, and go over the presentation with your director and/or the principals who will be making the announcement.

- Call, fax, or messenger media alerts to the daybooks of the various wire services and the assignment desks of TV and radio stations on your media list.

Day of the Event

- Do a walk-through of the facility. Make sure that signs directing the media to the proper room are in place, that you have clearly identified the people who will be sitting at the dais or lecturn by name and title, that you have the logo or name of your organization prominently displayed where television cameras can pick it up, and that the microphones are working.

- Make any last-minute calls.
- Get your media materials ready for delivery by messenger, as previously determined.
- Sign in all media representatives who show up.
- Arrange for someone to answer your office phone in case anyone gets lost or forgets where the conference is.
- Hand out news kits.
- Messenger materials to reporters who said they would attend but didn't. Then call and ask whether they require additional materials.
- Have your photographer drop off photos at the wire services and media outlets that have requested them. Print extra photos for later use.

Day After the Event

- Follow up with all those who attended to determine what other kinds of materials they may need.
- If the event made it to television, analyze the coverage to determine whether there are other ways to capitalize on it. Are there other story angles that can be exploited?
- Prepare media mailings with captioned photos. These probably will be best received by the trade and special interest media in your particular field.
- Alert important supporters and other concerned parties to the fact that your story was covered by the media.
- Consider how and to whom you might want to distribute the press clips. Can they be repackaged into a brochure or special mailing?
- Plan the next step in your overall publicity campaign. How can you gain additional exposure for your message?
- Finally, if the turnout was light, try to figure out why.

HARVARD MEDICAL SCHOOL
DEPARTMENT OF SOCIAL MEDICINE

Contact: Karen Borack/Patricia Garrison
             M Booth & Associates
             212/481-7000

* * * MEDIA ADVISORY * * *

**FINDINGS OF FIRST-EVER SURVEY OF WORLD MENTAL HEALTH
TO BE PRESENTED AT U.N. BRIEFING, MAY 15**

WHAT: The findings of a groundbreaking study of mental health in low-income
             nations will be presented at a special briefing at the United Nations. The
             three-year study--conducted by a team of experts from 30 nations looks
             at a broad range of issues, such as domestic violence, addiction, suicide,
             and exploitation of children. For example:

  *   Suicide, which accounts for roughly 1.6% of the world's
             mortality, is the one of the top causes of death among young
             people aged 15-24; for example, 62.3 per 100,000 in Sri Lanka
             and 21.3 per 100,000 in China;
  *   Pakistan, where heroin was introduced less than 20 years ago,
             now has the highest reported per capita usage of that drug in the
             world, with one in every 19 males consuming it regularly;
  *   Domestic violence is rampant worldwide: more than 61% of all
             women in Mexico are physically abused by their husbands; and
             50% of women living in Bangkok's largest slum are beaten
             regularly;
  *   The total number of cases of schizophrenia in low-income
             societies will increase from 16.7 million in 1985 to 24.4 million in
             the year 2000;
  *   As many as 90% of epileptics go untreated in certain Asian and
             African nations, because low-cost, anti-convulsive medication is
             not made available.

WHEN: **Monday, May 15, 1995**
             11:00 A.M. - Media Briefing

WHERE: Room 226 Secretariat Building, United Nations, New York

-2-

WHO: Dr. Arthur Kleinman, chair, Dept. of Social Medicine, Harvard Medical School, Boston, Massachusetts
Prof. Veena Das, Delhi School of Economics, University of Delhi, India
Dr. Julio Frenk, Fundacion Mexicana Para la Salud, Mexico
Dr. Miriam Were, UNFPA, Addis Ababa, Ethiopia
Dr. Sylvia Kaaya, University of Dar es Salaam, Tanzania
Dr. J.A. Costa e Silva, director, Division of Mental Health, World Health Organization
Dr. David Hamburg, president, Carnegie Corporation of New York

PLEASE NOTE: At 9:45 A.M. the panel will brief the Secretary General and other members of the international community in Conference Room 2. Accredited Media are welcome to observe this briefing.

Background: <u>*World Mental Health: Problems and Priorities in Low-Income Nations*</u> *is a systematic analysis of the burden of suffering imposed by mental and behavioral health problems on low-income societies in Africa, Asia, Latin America, and the Middle East. Its release marks the beginning of a campaign to focus world attention on what has been described as a "largely unheralded crisis in world mental health." An international call for action will be presented at a special briefing for U.N. Secretary General Boutros Boutros-Ghali and leaders from the international community.*

<u>*World Mental Health*</u> *is published by Oxford University Press. The study was supported by the Carnegie Corporation of New York, the John D. and Catherine T. MacArthur Foundation, the Rockefeller Foundation, and the Milbank Memorial Fund.*

PLEASE NOTE: For UN Accreditation Call 212/963-6934

# # #

APA·PPI

ASIAN PACIFIC AMERICAN
PUBLIC POLICY INSTITUTE

A **LEAP** Organization

■

327 East Second Street
Suite 226
Los Angeles, CA
90012-4210
213-485-1422
FAX 213-485-0050

■

CONTACT: Emily Whitfield/M Booth & Associates
212/481-7000

**EMBARGOED FOR RELEASE
9:30 A.M. E.S.T., WEDNESDAY, MAY 18, 1994**

MEDIA ADVISORY

**FIRST PROFILE OF ASIAN PACIFIC AMERICANS' STRUGGLES,
SUCCESSES IN U.S. ECONOMY:**

Spectacular Achievements of Fastest-Growing Segment of Population
Shadowed by Poverty, Glass Ceiling and Discrimination

WHAT: News conference and briefing to release **The State of Asian Pacific America: Economic Diversity, Issues & Policies**, the nation's first major analysis of Asian Pacific Americans' role in the U.S. economy. The report comes from LEAP's Asian Pacific American Public Policy Institute and the UCLA Asian American Studies Center.

An in-depth look at the areas of **high technology, health care, work force policies, enclave economies and welfare reform.**

WHEN: Wednesday, May 18, 1994, 9:30 - 11:00 a.m. (9:00 a.m. for coffee)

WHERE: National Press Club, Lisagor/White Rooms, 13th floor
14th Street and "F" Streets, NW, Washington, D.C.

WHO: .   **Paul M. Ong**, Ph.D., a nationally recognized demographics expert and editor/co-author of the report

.   **Don T. Nakanishi**, Ph.D., director of the UCLA Asian American Studies Center

.   **J.D. Hokoyama**, President and Executive Director, Leadership Education for Asian Pacifics, Inc.

.   Representative **Norman Y. Mineta** (D-CA, 15th Dist.)
.   Representative **Patsy T. Mink** (D-HI, 2nd Dist.)
.   Representative **Robert A. Underwood** (D-Guam)

- more -

Leadership Education
for Asian Pacifics, Inc.

HIGHLIGHTS FROM <u>THE STATE OF ASIAN PACIFIC AMERICA</u>:
<u>ECONOMIC DIVERSITY, ISSUES & POLICIES</u>

"THE HAVES AND HAVE-NOTS"

Long Work Hours, High Risk, Narrow Profit Margins -- But Limited Success

- Asian Pacific American entrepreneurship has increased by 973% since 1972

- Eleven percent of all Asian Pacific Americans are self-employed -- of that number, 85% are immigrants

- Asian Pacific American entrepreneurs accounted for 2.6% of all firms in 1987, yet only 1.7% of all receipts

- One-third of the self-employed are in the highly competitive, marginally profitable retail sector -- most commonly, restaurants

The Glass Ceiling and Discrimination -- Are We Treating Asian Pacific Americans Like "Hi-Tech Coolies?"

- Immigrants account for 46% of Asian Pacific American scientists and engineers

- Asian Pacific Americans are more likely to work in research and have a lower probability than white males of holding higher-paying management positions

- A "reverse brain drain" could sap critical talent, as scientists and engineers are lured to countries that offer better opportunities for leadership, advancement

Southeast Asians Trapped on Welfare

- Between 1975 and 1991, over one million Southeast Asian refugees migrated to the U.S.; today, Southeast Asians have the highest welfare dependency rate of any racial or ethnic group in the nation

- While Southeast Asians comprise only 13% of the total Asian Pacific American population, they account for up to 87% of all Asian Pacific Americans on welfare

- Limited English language and education are obstacles

Doctoring Discrimination: Health Care Professionals Shunted to Inner-City Hospitals

- Asian Pacific Americans represent nearly 11% of the nation's practicing physicians, yet they are consistently underrepresented in management positions

- Asian Pacific American medical professionals are highly visible in four of the largest municipal hospital systems -- New York (21%), Los Angeles (28%), San Francisco/Oakland (24%), and Chicago (13%)

- A study of three major public hospitals in Los Angeles revealed that, while Asian Pacific Americans comprise 34% of all professionals (physicians and nurses) and 28% of all supervisors, only 12% hold management positions

- as visual accompaniment for public-service announcements or as a component in slide/script features. Slides intended for use on television should be horizontal in format, with the subject centered in the frame.

The use of color transparencies—usually 46mm or more—generally is restricted to cover illustrations and full-page spreads, where their comparative expense is justified by the need for detail and crisp resolution. News magazines often use such shots on their "people" pages, mainly for celebrities, in which case they should appear to be spontaneous and be technically perfect—well-lit, sharply focused, and richly colored. News magazines usually insist on an exclusive when dealing with this kind of shot—another reason not to waste funds mass-producing color.

Often, the best approach to use with a transparency is to "offer color." This simply means providing an editor with a description of the shot's format, dominant colors, orientation (vertical or horizontal), and subject matter (i.e., who is pictured and what are they pictured doing). Here's a fictional example:

> "35mm slides available: vertical shots of Donald and Marla Trump at the Plaza Hotel handing an oversized check to the head of the Muscular Dystrophy Association as Jerry Lewis looks on. One end of the check is held by the head of the Association and the other by the Trumps."

If you have photos of a late-breaking story that are appropriate for the "people" pages of one of the major news magazines, you can send the entire roll of film to the magazine's photo editor accompanied by a release and descriptions of those photos you think are of interest. Don't forget to include your name, the name of your organization, and a telephone number(s) where you can be reached.

Photo Stories

It's possible to create a publicity mailing that consists only of photos. Such a mailing may include a single picture, a two- or three-up on one print, or a set of prints accompanied by a common caption or set of captions. Without a firm commitment from an editor, however, it may not be worth the time, money, and effort required to create a photo essay on spec.

On the other hand, for major benefits and other stories where your local paper has agreed to do a spread, the photo-essay approach is ideal. Local papers, and in particular weeklies, are always eager to print local

"Without a firm commitment from an editor . . . it may not be worth the time, money, and effort required to create a photo essay on spec."

residents' names, and the opportunity to print a picture is an added bonus. If the picture is something other than a headshot, you may well have a sale.

Captions

As a general rule, captions should be treated as leads, identifying all the important players pictured (and, in some cases, those not pictured as well) in two or three lines. Be sure to use directional tags (e.g., "left to right," "bottom row," "clockwise from the top") or some other device to specifically identify each person in the shot.

Include the name, address, and telephone number of your organization, as well as the name of a contact person and some reference to a date—either the date the picture was taken or the date the event took place. (See page 116 for an example.)

If you're sending machine prints from copy negatives, a caption, or *cutline,* can be burned or stripped in as the photo is being copied at virtually no extra cost. If you require a large number of machine prints, adding a cutline to a photo neg can also save you time. If, on the other hand, you're only sending out a few photos, don't bother.

Coverage

To ensure coverage of your event by freelance photographers who sell to news organizations, send a photo memo—an advisory to photo editors— a few days before the event. As is the case with TV assignment editors, photo assignment editors work on short lead times, blocking out staff time on a daily, rather than weekly or monthly, basis.

In your advisory, be sure to include the time your event is scheduled to start, the photo opportunity that will be available, the personalities who will be on hand, and why those personalities are doing what they'll be doing. Be as descriptive as possible about the kind of shot that will be available, and mention whether it lends itself to black-and-white or color. Include a contact name, address, and telephone number.

Taking Better Pictures

Many nonprofits rely on their staff to produce quality publicity photographs. Below are some helpful hints for taking better pictures, what to look for in a good picture, and how to make photo selections for brochures and publicity mailings.

"To ensure coverage of your event by freelance photographers who sell to news organizations, send a photo memo—an advisory to photo editors—a few days before the event."

Contact: **Karen Borack**
              212/481-7000

For: **Inwood House**

FOR IMMEDIATE RELEASE

NEW YORK, NY, June 8, 1994 -- WNBC-TV co-anchor Carol Jenkins (left) introducing Jeanne Moutassamy-Ashe (right) at today's Inwood House Gala, where Ms. Moutassamy-Ashe received the Inwood House Iphigene Ochs Sulzberger Award for Contributions to Family Life for her role in helping parents learn to talk to their children about AIDS.

The Gala benefited Teen Choice, Inwood House's pregnancy and AIDS prevention, sexuality education and counseling program which reaches over 5,000 New York City public school students.

Inwood House, a nonprofit agency, provides substitute living care and comprehensive services to single, pregnant young women and adolescent mothers and their children.

###

1. Try to get gestures into your photos; finger pointing, waving, and other hand movements can add action to otherwise static photos.

2. Think about the composition of your photos. How does the subject of the shot relate to his or her surroundings? Does that relationship make sense? Can you alter the frame and clarify that relationship by shifting your position? Is there a natural, more effective frame within the picture itself?

3. Good shots are those you watch and wait for.

4. Think about contrasts when taking a picture—old and young, smiling and crying, active and passive; they can add drama as well as interest to a photo.

5. With clichéd subject material—the ribbon-cutting ceremony, the dancing couple, the doctor examining a patient—variety in the expressions of your subjects can make a difference.

6. Use vantage point, frame, and light to simplify your pictures. The photographer always takes a shot from a particular vantage point. By moving closer or shifting the vantage point optically (i.e., changing lenses), you can often simplify and strengthen a picture.

7. Focusing on a single subject with a longer lens can enhance the impact of a photo.

8. For portraits, candid close-ups using the available light are usually the most effective.

9. At awards presentations, keep the picture simple and tight. Limit the subject matter to the people actually involved in the presentation, and never have more than three people in a shot. Keep your subjects' shoulders touching and keep them away from walls.

"Think about the composition of your photos. How does the subject of the shot relate to his or her surroundings?"

Clipping Services

Now that you've learned how to generate publicity, your final task is learning how to keep track of it. Clipping services monitor major (and, often, minor) media outlets and send you *clips* of any stories involving your organization. The average cost for such a service is $300 to $350 per month, and $1.00 to $1.50 per clip. (In radio and television, 10 words is considered a clip.) The above pricing applies to national searches. You can reduce your costs, however, by specifying more limited searches, both by reach (i.e., one state, five states, etc.) and by outlet.

4 Advertising— A Primer

"A public relations practitioner who does not understand the history, the uses, the techniques and the value of advertising is simply not equipped to perform all of his job."
—John Orr Young
co-founder of Young & Rubicam Advertising,
in *Lesley's Public Relations Handbook*

The essential difference between advertising and publicity is control of the message. Advertisers can determine what is said, how it is said, and where it is said. They can precisely position a product or service in the marketplace. Publicists, on the other hand, create and shape stories by working through the media. Because publicists must work with reporters and editors, their control of the message is limited.

For the purposes of most nonprofits, this distinction not only holds true, it is also a good place to start any discussion of the values and uses of advertising. Nonprofit managers whose groups lack large budgets too often and too quickly dismiss the idea of advertising, thereby limiting their dealings with the media to publicity. From a public relations perspective, *both* advertising and publicity are valid and useful communications techniques. Even for groups with severely limited funds, there are occasions when well-considered advertising and well-timed publicity are entirely appropriate and called for.

Indeed, advertising is an option most nonprofits should consider when developing an overall communications strategy. Performing arts groups, for example, must rely on a combination of critical reviews, features, performance listings, and paid advertising to build sales at the box office. Where a single technique does not succeed, several in concert can work to attract audiences.

Nonprofits outside the art world have also stepped up their advertising. Colleges and universities routinely tout courses and degrees—even on television—to attract students. Advocacy groups have long used advertising to draw attention to public issues or rally support for a cause. Many social service organizations have adopted advertising to find new clients. And nonprofits of all types and persuasions have mounted effective public-service campaigns.

The conclusion all these nonprofits have reached is that advertising can enhance existing media and communications efforts. When advertising is supported by an aggressive publicity program, it can leverage funding, sell programs and products, raise public awareness and understanding of issues, and create goodwill. It can add a new dimension to a group's communications program and provide increased flexibility in how an organization reaches its public.

"Most nonprofits should examine the possibility of public-service advertising. . . ."

It goes without saying that advertising is expensive. Creative costs, production costs, and media costs can quickly overwhelm what many public interest groups budget for an entire year's program. Most nonprofits should examine the possibility of public-service advertising (in which the media donates the space or time) as an alternative to paid advertising. And every nonprofit considering an ad campaign should keep the following in mind and be prepared to make some choices up front.

1. Advertising asking for donations often doesn't raise enough to cover the cost of the ad space. Don't count on recouping your expenses with new donations. Although advertising can create a favorable environment for fundraising, bolster a coordinated direct-mail program, reinforce a publicity campaign, or build excitement for a special event, it won't, by itself, raise money.

2. Effective advertising is built on an understanding of a product, a service, or an idea. The better that understanding, the better the advertising. Knowledge about an organization or service is best gained through careful study. There is simply no substitute for all the reading, interviewing, talking, and thinking that must be done to know a subject

well. Board members, staff, volunteers, and clients are good places to start your research.

3. Celebrities can be helpful in attracting attention and securing media placement. A well-known face, voice, or personality adds credibility to almost any message. The use of celebrities in public-service advertising can also leverage attention in the media among those who will decide whether or not to run your spots.

4. Think big. Too many campaigns have failed because the ideas were too small for the expected return, or because the budget was too limited for what needed to be accomplished. Even when advertising is the right technique, its execution can fall short of a goal. How much to spend is a dilemma many nonprofit advertisers face. This is particularly true of smaller groups, which usually have to invest a healthy percentage of their budgets if they want to advertise. As the financial commitment rises, so do the expectations for the campaign. The question you have to ask is, Can we afford to buy the results we want? If the answer is no, either bolster complementary activities—publicity, special mailings, posters—to increase the value of the advertising, or drop the advertising component of the communications program altogether.

THE MECHANICS OF PAID SPACE

An advertiser is faced with the same variables as the public relations planner: audience, intended response, and timing. On one count, however—the relationship with the media—the advertiser's choices are different.

Newspapers

Newspapers across the nation significantly changed advertising formats in 1984, when they adopted a Standard Advertising Unit. The newer system replaced an often confusing selection of shapes and sizes and allowed advertisers to choose from standardized sizes. The standard, which was adopted by all daily newspapers in the U.S., created order out of what used to be a chaotic situation involving as many as 432 different measurements. The changeover also reduced production costs for display ads and made media purchases easier.

"A well-known face, voice, or personality adds credibility to almost any message."

Under the new system, most newspapers measure advertising in inches rather than lines of type. Rates, of course, vary enormously, depending on the paper and discount packages available. For example, many dailies give discounts to nonprofits, special-section advertisers, repeat advertisers, and advertisers who don't require special placement. A newspaper's display advertising department can fill you in on the details.

Radio and TV Ads

All 9,900 commercial television and radio stations in the U.S. offer time in standard blocks. Among the more common are the 10-, 20-, 30-, and 60-second spot. Radio and television ad rates generally are negotiable—certainly more so than is the case with print media. The price of a spot is determined by when it runs, the number of times it runs, and its length. Television rates also vary by station, program ratings, and time period. Your costs will be lower if your spot can be run whenever it fits in, or if it can be aired around a particular program, thereby targeting a particular audience. Station media representatives usually have detailed demographics showing which time periods attract which audiences. If you are selling tickets or promoting an issue, this kind of information is invaluable.

Spots on television or radio can be produced in advance or run live. For TV, an announcer can read copy as long as there is some visual element—a slide or series of slides—on the air. Or you can supply tape or film. Query each station on its specifications (1-, ¾, or ½-inch videotape or Beta).

For radio, ads can be produced on tape using a union announcer, music, and a rented studio, or as a script with the radio announcer reading copy on the air (120 to 150 words per minute). The advantage of a tape is that you know what it will sound like before it airs. In general, taped ads are more consistent and interesting than live spots.

Magazine Ads

Magazine ads are like newspaper ads, except that the lead times for them are much longer—up to three months or more in advance of publication. The ad sizes also relate to the layout of the page—full-page, half-page, quarter-page, etc. In addition, you can opt for *bleeds* (where the art runs all the way to the edge of the page), *double trucks* (facing full-page ads), and color.

Drop-in ads are often used by both magazines and newspapers as fillers. Usually involving nothing more than a name, logo, or slogan, they are sometimes sufficient to get a simple message across.

"Your costs will be lower if your spot can be run whenever it fits in, or if it can be aired around a particular program. . . ."

Billboards and Transit Advertising

Billboards offer advertisers standardized display panels in more than 9,000 locations across the country. Advertising in mass-transit locales such as buses and subways allows for cards of various shapes and sizes. The three basic cost elements—creating the campaign, executing it, and space rental—are the same. Both options are well suited for public-service announcements. Nonprofits should check with local transportation authorities for the name of the agency (often an outside firm) that handles the negotiations.

PUBLIC-SERVICE ADVERTISING

Although public-service advertising costs less than regular advertising, it's not necessarily free. First, there's the expense of creating the ad, which includes the costs associated with making basic strategic decisions about audiences and how to appeal to them. There's also the expense of producing the ad, including fees for photographers, graphic designers, typesetters, audio engineers, musicians, onscreen talent, and so on.

While some groups work closely with media outlets to reduce the production costs of advertising, such an arrangement is not always possible, in which case the costs must either be paid for out of pocket or through special fundraising appeals. And though there are clear savings related to public-service advertising when the media donates time or space, the hidden cost can be the loss of control over when the ads are used.

Of course, for many nonprofits the costs associated with retaining creative advertising minds and producing and placing any kind of advertising are prohibitive. For example, production expenses on a national public-service advertising program can run upwards of $150,000. Even local campaigns require the services of a typesetter, photographer, or film editor. More often than not, smaller groups simply do not have the funds, and the competition for resources within larger organizations effectively limits the use of paid advertising on a sustained basis.

The alternative is to get some or all of these media and production costs donated. Last year, the media contributed more than $1 billion (or approximately 2 percent of media time) for advertising that was in the public interest. In addition, agency managers, art directors, and copywriters gave freely of their time and expertise. Clearly, the benefits of donated services that accrue to nonprofits in the form of contributions, new volunteers, improved morale, or a better understanding of a particular problem can be enormous.

". . . though there are clear savings related to public-service advertising when the media donates time or space, the hidden cost can be the loss of control over when the ads are used."

SPECIAL HINTS FOR PLACING PSAs

- Listen to radio stations and watch television to get a feeling for the content of specific shows and the formats favored by different outlets. This will help you determine which stations are most appropriate as vehicles for your message. Consider the type of audience that is reached by different types of programming.

- Set up an appointment with whoever is responsible for a station's PSAs. Remember, it's that person's job to serve the community.

- When distributing spots to stations, include a cover letter and relevant promotional material explaining your program or campaign. The cover letter should contain your organization's address, zip code, telephone number (with area code), and the name of a person who can be contacted for more information.

- If there are specific dates for the start and/or conclusion of a program or campaign, clearly note them in the cover letter and on the spots themselves. Should changes occur that would in any way affect the accuracy of the spots that are being aired, notify all stations immediately of the changes.

- When preparing PSAs, be sure that accurate organizational identification is included in every spot.

- In certain circumstances, you may want to avoid using popular radio or television personalities in spots prepared for a local market, especially if that individual's show is aired in a competing time slot. For similar reasons, avoid political candidates as spokespersons.

- Enclose a copy of your organization's Internal Revenue Service determination letter and any other proof of your tax-exempt status.

- Most stations prefer 1-inch video over ¾-inch, ½-inch, or Beta. Play it safe and check in advance or offer a combination.

- Film prints or tape recordings supplied to stations should have the best production values you can muster. The more professional the production and the "cleaner" the tape or film stock used, the greater your chances of acceptance.

- It is important to provide feedback to broadcasters. A letter describing the benefits you derived from the exposure they gave your spots is *always* appreciated.

It is not every nonprofit, however, that can persuade a newspaper publisher or television station manager to promote its programs or causes. The media is inundated with requests for free space, free time, and free help. As a result, formal guidelines covering the content and format of such advertising have been developed. On the creative side, the advertising industry has taken a similar approach, with the Ad Council acting on a national basis as the public-service arm for the industry.

For groups considering a public-service campaign, it is always a good idea to query the media as well as any contacts in the advertising industry to see what kind of help is available without charge. Most radio and television stations have a community-relations coordinator or public-service director to deal with such requests. In the print media, contact the publisher's office. Finding an advertising agency that is willing to donate its time to create a professional campaign can be more problematic, particularly for nonprofit groups without personal contacts among agency heads, copywriters, or art directors, in which case local industry associations may be able to provide you with leads.

Once creative help is forthcoming (either from an agency or from freelancers), it's important to remember that there will likely be production costs to cover. These include type and artwork fees on print advertising; fees for professional narration, studio time, and release tapes for radio spots; and the cost of a camera crew, editors' fees, and release prints for television spots. Such costs can mount quickly, even for local campaigns.

For those who cannot foot such out-of-pocket expenses, a do-it-yourself approach is in order. For print media, the process is similar to

"For groups considering a public-service campaign, it is always a good idea to query the media as well as any contacts in the advertising industry to see what kind of help is available without charge."

preparing any printed piece (see Chapter 2, "Developing Informational Materials"). There's a different set of ground rules for electronic media, however.

In general, the PSA is a precisely timed message that can be 10-, 20-, 30-, or 60-seconds long (some groups and media outlets are experimenting with PSAs up to two minutes in length). These messages are aired during commercial breaks, generally during off-peak hours. Even so, they reach a considerable audience and competition for airtime is keen.

Because of the enormous number of local groups asking for PSA time, most stations prefer to use shorter spots. Short spots allow stations to accommodate a greater number of community organizations in the time they allot for PSAs. Therefore, you should design your spots to convey a simple, direct message. As with other types of advertising, PSAs should elicit a particular response or action from the audience—to use a service, to order a product, to call for information, or to request a brochure. In a TV PSA, the message should be reinforced with visuals—slides, film, or videotape. Slides for TV PSAs should be 35mm color, horizontally composed and centered, and have visual appeal. (Radio spots should be recorded at 7-½ inches per second.)

Keep the script for your spot simple. Make every word count and watch out for words that carry a hidden meaning. Does the message you're trying to convey come out sounding negative? Is the spot clear about what the audience should do? Are your organization's name and telephone number announced clearly? Take the time to say exactly what you want to say, and no more.

Scripts should be read aloud and timed with a stopwatch. Use the following as a rule of thumb:

> 10 seconds — 10–15 words
> 20 seconds — 35–40 words
> 30 seconds — 55–65 words
> 60 seconds — 120–125 words

To determine what length your spot should be, check with the media outlet that has agreed to run the spot and find out what their requirements are. Not every station uses every type of spot. You may want to produce several spots, each a different length, so they can be worked into available time slots more easily. All should convey the same message, however. (See pages 127–129 for examples.)

"As with other types of advertising, PSAs should elicit a particular response or action from the audience. . . ."

ARCHITECTURAL HERITAGE YEAR

Public Service Announcement

:60 Radio

CASTLES RISING FROM CRAGGY ROCKS ... MOVIE HOUSES LAVISH AS A PALACE

... MOUNTAIN "COTTAGES" WITH FIFTY BEDROOMS AND FIFTEEN BATHS ... AN

OFFICE BUILDING SHAPED LIKE A FLATIRON. IS THIS AN AMUSEMENT PARK? A

FANTASY LAND? NO, THEY'RE EXAMPLES OF THE WONDERFUL ARCHITECTURE

OF NEW YORK STATE -- A SAMPLING OF BUILDINGS AND STRUCTURES OF THE

PAST THAT CONTINUE TO BEAUTIFY OUR TOWNS, CITIES, AND COUNTRYSIDES

TODAY. THROUGHOUT THIS YEAR, NEW YORKERS ACROSS THE STATE ARE

CELEBRATING THAT RICH LEGACY AS PART OF ARCHITECTURAL HERITAGE

YEAR ... TAKING A CLOSER LOOK AT THE MAGNIFICENT, RARE, UNUSUAL, AND

JUST PLAIN BEAUTIFUL ARCHITECTURE OF ANOTHER AGE -- MUCH OF IT RIGHT

HERE IN OUR OWN COMMUNITY. THE PRESERVATION LEAGUE OF NEW YORK

STATE, SPONSORS OF ARCHITECTURAL HERITAGE YEAR, HOPES YOU'LL WANT

TO BE PART OF THE CELEBRATION. THERE ARE EVENTS AND ACTIVITIES

SCHEDULED FROM NOW TO DECEMBER. IF YOU'D LIKE TO KNOW MORE,

CONTACT THE PRESERVATION LEAGUE OF NEW YORK STATE, 307 HAMILTON

STREET, ALBANY, NEW YORK 12210.

###

ANTHONY MICHAEL HALL PSA   :30

MUSIC	VOICE
"DON'T YOU FORGET ABOUT ME"	I'M MICHAEL ANTHONY HALL ASKING YOU TO JOIN ME IN HELPING THE STARVING PEOPLE OF AFRICA. I'M WORKING WITH CATHOLIC RELIEF SERVICES BECAUSE THEY'RE RIGHT THERE IN AFRICA BRINGING IN TONS OF FOOD AND EMERGENCY MEDICAL CARE. AND THEY'RE HELPING THE AFRICAN PEOPLE TO BUILD FOR THEIR FUTURE.
	CATHOLIC RELIEF SERVICES NEEDS ALL OF US. SO PLEASE, WRITE TO ME, ANTHONY MICHAEL HALL, CARE OF CATHOLIC RELIEF SERVICES, POST OFFICE BOX 2045, CHURCH STREET STATION, NEW YORK, NEW YORK, 10008. THANK YOU.
Music fade out.	

```
ANTHONY MICHAEL HALL PSA   :60
```

<div style="display: flex;">

<div>

VIDEO

Scene: Anthony
Michael Hall stands
with a group of
friends outside the
high school gym
before a big dance;
music plays from
someone's radio. He
separates from his
buddies to talk to
the camera.

He walks out the
door and down the
front steps, past
clusters of students
who slowly begin
listening to his
message.

CU of Michael
looking into the
camera.

Dissolve to CRS
address.

Fade to black.

</div>

<div>

AUDIO

YOU KNOW I GUESS IT'S PRETTY EASY TO GET
WRAPPED UP IN YOUR OWN WORLD SOMETIMES.
I MEAN THERE'S A LOT HAPPENING FOR ALL
OF US RIGHT NOW. THERE'S A LOT OF
PRESSURE. AND THERE'S A LOT OF FUN.
BUT THERE ARE OTHER THINGS THAT REALLY
CONCERN ALL OF US -- NO MATTER HOW OLD
WE ARE. ONE OF THESE THINGS IS BEING
ABLE TO HELP THOSE WHO DESPERATELY NEED
FOOD AND EMERGENCY MEDICAL CARE. THAT'S
WHY I DECIDED TO DO SOMETHING. IF WE
CAN FEED PEOPLE NOW AND DO ALL WE CAN TO
HELP AFRICAN FARMERS GROW THEIR OWN
FOOD, THEN PEOPLE MAY NEVER HAVE TO GO
HUNGRY AGAIN. I'M ANTHONY MICHAEL HALL
AND I'M HELPING CATHOLIC RELIEF SERVICES
BECAUSE THEY'RE RIGHT THERE IN AFRICA,
BRINGING IN TONS OF FOOD AND MEDICINE TO
HELP SAVE LIVES NOW. AND THEY'RE
WORKING WITH THE AFRICAN PEOPLE TO HELP
THEM PLAN THEIR FUTURES. CATHOLIC
RELIEF SERVICES NEEDS ALL OF US. SO OF
YOU FEEL THE SAME WAY WE DO, PLEASE
WRITE TO ME, CARE OF CATHOLIC RELIEF
SERVICES, TODAY.

                CATHOLIC RELIEF SERVICES
                 ANTHONY MICHAEL HALL
                     P.O. BOX 2045
                 CHURCH STREET STATION
                 NEW YORK, NY 10008
```

</div>

</div>
```

5 Speaking Before the Public

One of the most effective ways for an organization to reach out to its important audiences is to address them face-to-face through speeches, roundtables, panel discussions, symposia, briefings, and lectures. The communication is direct, and the personality of the speaker can be used to promote an organization's mission and purpose as it can with no other promotional technique. More often than not, the give-and-take between audience and speaker proves invaluable.

For many nonprofits, public-speaking opportunities present themselves on a regular basis. Luncheon meetings, association gatherings, educational conferences, and annual meetings are but a few of the chances for organizational spokespersons to motivate the sympathetic and convince the skeptical. They are opportunities that should be sought and exploited.

FINDING AND RECRUITING SPOKESPERSONS

The role of the spokesperson in most nonprofits falls naturally to a board or staff member, whether the chair, president, executive director, or a program manager. Other nonprofits look beyond their staff and boards for dynamic, effective public speakers. Known experts in a given field, even Hollywood celebrities, frequently are called on to serve as spokespersons for institutions, special campaigns, even specific services. Other speakers, some of them volunteers, are recruited for their knowledge and understanding of a particular subject. What all good public speakers share, however, is an ability to cogently and compellingly present a case using a combination of facts, reason, passion, and charm.

TRAINING AND PREPARATION

Once a speaker has accepted an engagement, the credibility of the organization and the individual are at stake. The audience will expect to hear an expert on a given topic—someone who knows a field thoroughly and can explain subject matter that other people find to be complex and even unfathomable. To offer as a speaker someone who is less than an expert is to sacrifice an opportunity to make new converts. At worst, a bad speaker risks raising questions and doubts about an organization and its programs.

Unfortunately, those in positions where regular speaking comes with the job are not always skilled at what they do. This should come as no surprise. The best public speakers make the job look easy, when in fact it is quite difficult.

For example, self-confidence is no guarantee that a speaker will captivate his or her audience. Although a speaker may appear to be at ease at a podium, he or she may soon fall into odd speech patterns or display annoying personal mannerisms (rocking back and forth, nervous coughing) that detracts from the impact of his or her presentation. For these and other reasons, tips from a seasoned professional can be invaluable, and speakers should be encouraged to sit down with a pro, whether they believe they need it or not.

"To offer as a speaker someone who is less than an expert is to sacrifice an opportunity to make new converts."

MATTERS OF STYLE

While the personality of the speaker should shine through in every speech, there are several rules of thumb for anyone about to address an audience.

1. There is no substitute for spontaneity. Although a speech can be written out, it shouldn't be read and it shouldn't be memorized. Instead, rely on notes. Effective speakers think ideas, not words.

2. A speaker has to be heard. If a microphone is called for, make sure it works. Although we can't all be trained actors, our voices need to project. Speak slowly and enunciate.

3. A speech should reflect the personality of the speaker. It should be personal and conversational and make use of pronouns and contractions. The speaker should make eye contact with individual members of the audience as much as possible.

4. Short, simple sentences and clear ideas should be the order of the day. Use language that evokes images. Listeners need to know where a speaker is headed and where he or she has been. Repeat important information.

5. The most effective speakers always present a neat, well-groomed appearance. Don't overdress. Keep jewelry to a minimum.

6. Avoid mannerisms that distract—gazing at distant objects, pacing, rocking, coin jiggling, ear pulling, excessive throat clearing, and so on. A speaker's body language should express his or her desire to communicate and connect with the audience.

7. All speakers should anticipate and prepare for the probability of stage fright—particularly early on. Sometimes it helps to take a sip of water or a deep breath before you start. Audiences don't want to hear apologies; they want to be entertained and informed.

8. Too much practice can lead to diminishing returns, especially for the amateur. Remember, the more clearly you understand what you *want* to say, the less you'll have to worry about *how* you say it, and the more successful your speech will be.

"Effective speakers think ideas, not words."

LOGISTICAL ISSUES

In addition to program content, there is important information every speaker needs before mounting a podium. A tip sheet outlining logistical information and specific audience considerations should be included in any package of prepatory materials you supply to a speaker in the weeks leading up to a speech. Such a sheet should answer, or at least raise, some or all of the following questions:

- Who is in the audience?
- Where are they from?
- What is their average age?
- What is their reason for convening?
- What are their interests?
- Do they have certain political inclinations, prejudices, or leanings?
- Should certain topics be avoided?
- What is the purpose of the speech? What does the speaker hope to accomplish?
- What are the ground rules for the talk? How long should the speech be?
- Will there be time for questions and answers?
- How large is the room? Will there be a standing lectern? A dais? A stage? Are there audiovisuals or other props that can be used?

ORGANIZING A SPEAKERS' BUREAU

A speakers' bureau is usually composed of individuals who are able to tell an organization's story convincingly. These speakers, in consultation with staff or the director, should select several topics that are important to the group's overall communications objectives. What are the three or four things that your organization is emphasizing this year? What themes or messages do you want to impress upon supporters, potential supporters, and even your critics? The topics should be framed so that they catch a group's interest. Something as generic as "the environment" won't do. A specific viewpoint concerning the environment, something like "Surviving Tomorrow's Environmental Crises Today," adds punch to the topic and makes it easier to sell.

Once your speakers and topics are in order, select those community, business, and professional associations that would make ideal audiences. Who are the influential leaders of the community? Who are your potential supporters? To which clubs do your organization's critics (if you have any) belong? Which groups are consistently covered by the media? Where

"A speakers' bureau is usually composed of individuals who are able to tell an organization's story convincingly."

can you make the biggest splash? Each group you decide to approach will have a program chairperson who books speakers for regular meetings or special events. Either call or write this person and offer your organization's speakers and topics.

A brochure or form letter listing your speakers' backgrounds and affiliations can be helpful. A form reply postcard or other type of self-addressed correspondence form should be enclosed to make bookings easier. Be sure to state when your speakers are available (days, evenings, weekends).

Once a speaker is engaged, a confirmation letter to the sponsor reconfirming the date, time, topic, length of presentation, and any other pertinent details should be sent. A biography of the speaker and background information about the speaker's topic should also be enclosed with the letter.

WRITING A SPEECH

> *"Speechwriting is to writing as Muzak is to music. . . ."*
> —Aram Bakshian, Jr., former director of
> speechwriting for President Reagan

> *"Speechwriting is the reverse of newspaper writing. You put the important things near the end in a speech."*
> —Anthony Dolan, a speechwriter for President Reagan

There is as much advice on how to write and deliver a good speech as there are good and bad speeches and good and mediocre speakers. And it's no wonder. If there's one thing that causes most of us to break into a cold sweat, it's an assignment to write or deliver a speech. It's also no wonder that in the corporate and political worlds, the good speechwriter earns more and is held in higher esteem than just about anyone else on the communications staff.

More people remember John F. Kennedy for his effectiveness as a speaker than for what he said. We remember ringing phrases but not necessarily entire passages. And while most of us can't remember his exact words, we do recall that he had a magical way of saying them.

Don't expect that all the speeches you write or deliver will help you win an election. Be circumspect in what you want to accomplish. As you would with any good written piece, map out what you want to say, how you want to begin, and where you want to end up.

"If there's one thing that causes most of us to break into a cold sweat, it's an assignment to write or deliver a speech."

*"Keep your
opening short,
sweet, and to
the point."*

The Opening

Just about everyone agrees that the opening and the close of a speech are
its most important elements. A good opening captures your audience,
while, as dramatically as possible, a good close leaves it to ponder your
main point.

Speechwriting is, after all, dramatic writing. The purpose of a speech
is to inform, to convince, to persuade, to defend, to entertain. It's a tough
assignment, and all the tools available to the speaker—body language,
voice, language, props—should contribute to the overall effect of the
speech.

Most professional speechwriters start with a *grabber*—one line,
phrase, anecdote, quote, or joke that grabs the audience's attention. In
effect, it lets the audience know that this is going to be a speech worth
listening to. Of the different kinds of openers, however, be especially
careful of quotes and humor. Quotes often seem like the easy way out.
Humor, if it's out of place or your delivery is not quite on a par with
David Letterman's, too often falls flat.

Here are some examples of effective grabbers:

> You know, this year, Sakowitz's Department Store in Texas—
> the one that always comes out with those outrageously priced
> Christmas gifts—had something really expensive in its cata-
> logue: a hospital bed. The cost: about $80,000.
> *—from a speech on the high cost of hospital care*

> Don't be surprised if the next time you see Leonardo da Vinci
> it's on the unemployment line. Maybe not yesterday's da
> Vinci—because he had his government supporting his creative
> genius. But tomorrow's da Vinci—the creative genius who
> today does not have his government behind him.
> *—from a speech about the importance of federal
> support for the arts*

Keep your opening short, sweet, and to the point. Writing a good
speech is like writing a good feature article, except that you have to pay
even more attention to your opening and your close, to the rhythm and
sound of your words, and to the formidable task of saying those words
in a limited period of time.

The Middle

It is usually a good idea to outline what you want to say after your
opening. Examine the main points you want to make and give some

indication of how they can be logically supported. It's also a good idea to limit the number of points you want to make. There's no reason to tell an audience everything you know, or more than they wanted to know, about a particular subject. An effective speech makes a point or two; don't try for more.

A good way of transitioning into the body of your speech is to pose a series of questions. Imagine that you're having a one-way dialogue with your audience and the questions you raise are the questions the listeners want raised.

Avoid connecting phrases like "Now let's talk about . . . ," or "This leads me to . . . ," or ". . . and so on." A speech is not an outline or list; it should be a cohesive, intelligent, and well-paced presentation.

Throughout the speech, make a conscious effort to use triads—groupings of grammatical elements in units of three. Remember "faith, hope, and charity" and "friends, Romans, countrymen"? According to *The Executive Speaker* newsletter, triads can help to outline your points and give you a way to continue or end.

The Close

If there's any part of a speech that may need extra work, it's usually the close. While a good close should summarize the main points you've made, it should go beyond a mere summary or reiteration and leave your audience with something memorable.

The close should contain language that stirs your audience to action, causes them to agree with you, or evokes an emotional response. A good close should use strong words and avoid punchless phrases such as "In closing," "Lastly," "Finally," or "In sum." Think of the last sentence or two as your close. Will it rouse your audience into applause? If it won't, try to come up with something that will.

Look at the way television newsman Ted Koppel uses unequivocal language and powerful imagery suggested by his own medium to urge a young audience to eschew ambivalence, cynicism, and materialism:

> I caution you, as one who performs daily on that flickering altar, to set your sights beyond what you can see. There is true majesty in the concept of an unseen power which can neither be measured nor weighed. There is harmony and inner peace to be found in following a moral compass that points in the same direction, regardless of fashion or trend. There is hope that if we can only set our course according to man's finest aspirations, we can achieve what we all want and that we can have it without diminishing our neighbor's share. Peace! May it come to your generation.

"There's no reason to tell an audience everything you know, or more than they wanted to know, about a particular subject."

SELF-HELP TIPS ON DELIVERING A SPEECH

- Keep your audience in mind. Know how many people are out there, who they are, and why they've come. If nothing else, it will help you during the question-and-answer period and give you a greater sense of why you are up there.

- As for stage fright, recall Mark Twain's comforting words: "Just remember, they don't expect much." And, according to writer and editor George Plimpton, your anxiety may actually help you do a better job.

- Practice aloud—and often—in front of a mirror; it will help you make eye contact. A good rule of thumb is to practice a speech at least three times before you present it.

- Try not to depend on a script.

- Keep the tone of your voice strong and confident. Remember, you're supposed to be the expert.

- If there's a question-and-answer period, don't be afraid to say, "I don't know the answer to that question; I'll try to find out for you."

- If you suddenly forget your lines or lose your place, try restating your last statement, summarizing what you just said, or asking for questions before you continue. Any one of these ploys will serve to jog your memory and give you time to find those missing lines.

- Relax—it isn't an exam. Be conversational, but make sure you have some notes, if not the entire text of your speech, written out. Try writing out the most important points and then talking around them. If

> you can do that, great. If not, try to inject some extemporaneity into your notes. Remember, it's a talk, not a lecture.
>
> - Only use audiovisual materials if you have to. Although technically oriented talks usually require slides or transparencies, graphics can detract from the flow of a speech, making it seem like a term paper.
>
> - Make eye contact with your audience. Try to gauge their reaction to what you have to say and give them a chance to react.
>
> - Don't try to say too much. Your 15 minutes at the podium is part of a larger communications picture, not the entire picture. And as with any communications vehicle, when in doubt, cut it out.

Speechwriting should not be done in a vacuum. With the exception of canned speeches (which, as much as possible, should be reworked to suit the individual speaker), every speech you or someone in your organization writes should be created for a particular person. The speechwriter should be familiar with the speaker's speech patterns, phrasing, and favorite anecdotal materials.

In many ways, good speechwriting is like poetry. Once you capture the speaker's rhythms, the language should flow. Writing a speech is a singular feat. It requires literacy, intelligence, and creativity. It is one of the most difficult assignments a writer can be given and, when pulled off successfully, one of the most rewarding. For the writer it is a challenge, an opportunity to become immersed in a subject. For the person delivering the speech, it is an opportunity to take the mask off and literally talk to the issues—to move outside the sheltered shell of an organization. And for the organization, it is an opportunity to meet the public head on.

An irresistible close to this section is provided by humorist Art Buchwald, from a speech he made at Catholic University in Washington, D.C.:

> Now, I could have said something profound today, but you would have forgotten it in ten minutes; so I chose to give this kind of speech instead so that 20 years from now when your

"The speechwriter should be familiar with the speaker's speech patterns, phrasing, and favorite anecdotal materials."

children ask you what you did on graduation day, you can proudly say, "I laughed."

PUBLICITY ON SPEECHES

Many speeches, if they are worth giving, are worth publicizing. It is incumbent upon public relations professionals to publicize speeches in the local press—to prepare news releases and media alerts announcing the speech, to invite the media to attend, and, finally, to make phone calls and issue a day-of release summarizing the major points made in the speech. Include copies of the speech with the release, if possible.

A speech can be embargoed until after it is delivered. While it is often important to distribute copies of the speech beforehand in order to receive media coverage, it is always possible that some last-minute hitch will prevent the speaker from addressing a group or will necessitate changes in his or her planned remarks. Guard against embarrassment, or worse, by putting on top of the speech (and noting in any conversations with media representatives) the words EMBARGOED UNTIL _____ (fill in the time or date when you think it will be safe to quote the speech in detail).

When you distribute a speech to the media, make certain the accompanying news release highlights the major facts about the speech. What is the topic of the speech, who delivered it, what are its main points, to whom was it delivered, when, and why? Quote liberally from the speech. Again, if the news release is issued after the speech is safely underway or finished, its top should be headed HOLD FOR RELEASE UNTIL _____.

If the speech is particularly important, you might want to package it in a specially designed brochure for mailing to supporters, potential supporters, media outlets, and other target groups. You might even try to have it reprinted in full or excerpted on the op-ed page of your local paper; or provide it to your congressional representative for inclusion in the *Congressional Record* as an address worth noting (in which case you can reprint the speech using that distinguished *CR* logo). Or you can submit the speech for consideration to a publication such as *Vital Speeches*.

Finally, speeches should be tape-recorded, if possible, for later transcription and use, as well as for analysis and constructive criticism of the speech's content and the speaker's style.

"When you distribute a speech to the media, make certain the accompanying news release highlights the major facts about the speech."

6 Special Events

Although most special events sponsored by nonprofit organizations—theater premieres and benefits, raffles and receptions, black-tie dinners—are for fundraising purposes, they do provide an opportunity for publicity and media coverage, especially if public relations is included in the planning and utilized during the events themselves.

There are other special events—building dedications and ribbon-cutting ceremonies, lectures and roundtables, exhibitions, awards ceremonies, parades—that are organized specifically around public relations goals. These kinds of events provide a good opportunity to publicize special aspects of an organization's work or its participation in the community it serves. Both kinds of events lend themselves to a multiplicity of organizational objectives and are classic examples of how public relations and fundraising work hand-in-hand.

As long as they are appropriate and well-planned, special events are suitable for nearly every kind of nonprofit organization. They can be on a grand scale if the venue and budget allow and there are enough people available to handle the work. But even on a smaller scale, they can benefit your organization.

To illustrate how fundraising and public relations activities can dovetail, consider Share Our Strength's highly successful "Taste of the Nation," the largest nationwide benefit for hunger relief. Over a ten-day period one year, 5,000 chefs in more than 100 cities prepared their specialties at food- and wine-tasting events. More than 60,000 guests

141

attended, and 100 percent of the ticket proceeds benefited the organization. Nationally, corporate sponsor American Express provided funding for the organizational and promotional expenses, while local sponsors covered similar expenses in their markets.

Each city created its own theme for its event. In Los Angeles the event became a gourmet food-tasting along Universal Studios' "Streets of the World." In Fort Lauderdale the event was themed "Tropical Fever." In Oklahoma City cooking classes and a country western dance spiced up the evening. And in New York City the elegant food- and wine-tasting was staged on two separate yachts.

Public relations goals were at the center of Share Our Strength's planning, and as a result the organization was successful in generating both national and local news. Nationally, the program was billed as the largest nationwide benefit for hunger relief, and as such was featured in newspapers such as *USA Today* and *The Christian Science Monitor*. At the local level, publicity was generated by the celebrity chefs who participated in each city. Photo opportunities and articles about local sponsors and beneficiaries of the program popped up in newspapers across the country. And because 70 percent of the funds raised in local markets stayed in those markets, the local news hook was even harder to resist.

"Taste of the Nation" is an example of the special event raised to art form. Such large-scale events are not uncommon, though more often than not these days organizations are being forced to reduce budgets and keep events simple.

If your organization finds itself in the same boat, consider staging something on a smaller scale, say a ribbon-cutting ceremony to dedicate a new facility, with community and foundation representatives on hand, or a lecture series or roundtable discussion. Such events are informational in nature and can be a valuable resource for beat reporters. At the same time, they provide your organization with a platform for communicating its message.

Regardless of the type of event you decide to stage, doing it right means knowing what you want to achieve and having the means to achieve it. The following is a list of questions you should consider before undertaking any special event, large or small.

"Regardless of the type of event you decide to stage, doing it right means knowing what you want to achieve and having the means to achieve it."

- What are your objectives? Do you want to generate publicity, bolster your fundraising efforts, address policy issues, improve relations with the community and local government, educate the public, attract new members, or just thank your existing members?

- Is an event the best way to accomplish any or all of these objectives? Is there a better and/or less expensive way? Would a news release, a paid ad, or a meeting accomplish the same thing?

- Is there an adequate budget to do the event right? Has every out-of-pocket expense been factored in? Space and equipment rentals? Catering? List development? Stationery, invitations, placecards, and postage? Telephone and facsimile follow-ups? Security? Media materials, including photocopying, printing, and production costs? Entertainment? Videotaping and/or photography? PA equipment?

- Will you end up spending more money on the event than you make? If so, do other benefits outweigh the net loss in revenue?

If you've considered all this and are still committed to going ahead with the event, your next step should be to develop a budget with all out-of-pocket expenses carefully itemized. Be sure to include a *contingency line* to give yourself some margin for unanticipated expenses, escalating costs, and miscalculations.

STAFF RECRUITMENT

Professional public relations staffers are integral to the success of special events where public visibility is an objective. Such professionals, along with other key program staff, should form the core planning group for this type of event.

In order to be judged a success, many events are important enough to require significant inputs of time and manpower. In such cases, it may be necessary to set up a volunteer committee to ensure that the myriad details are attended to. This committee should answer to a chairperson and, depending on the scope of the event, should be broken down into a number of subcommittees responsible for publicity, entertainment, ticket sales, media materials, follow-up, invitations, and so on.

In addition, the chair might want to appoint a steering committee—a small and carefully selected group that coordinates staff and volunteer activities. A counterpart staff member often sits on the steering committee to advise and ensure that plans are consistent with the organization's goals and other activities. The steering committee should create the master plan for the event and oversee the various assignments and time-tables as the event unfolds. If your board or organization has a public relations committee, a representative from it should be on the steering committee as well.

"Be sure to include a contingency line *to give yourself some margin for unanticipated expenses, escalating costs, and miscalculations."*

A final suggestion: For both publicity and organizational purposes, it can be a plus for your chairperson (or honorary chair) to be well known in the community. Among other benefits, a well-known chairperson will help sell tickets, attract high-profile volunteers, garner media attention, and lend cachet to the event.

COMMITTEE DESIGNATION

Organizing an event requires the careful coordination of dozens of people and activities. While specific organizational objectives may result in one aspect of your planning being emphasized over another, the success of any event ultimately hinges on good work in several areas.

Invitations

A committee will need to decide who is to be invited to the event, how they should be invited, and when the invitations should go out. Remember, your list should include representatives from the local (and national, when appropriate) media. For fundraising events, invitations are often more elaborate in design (and thus cost more) and sometimes include postpaid return cards as a way of boosting the response rate. (If you're staging a benefit, selling tickets is what it's all about.)

Materials and Equipment

Depending on the size of your event, everything from programs and menus to transportation and a decent sound system will have to be produced or arranged for. If the event is going to be covered by local television stations, you need to make sure there's ample room for the cameras and camera people and that there are enough outlets and an adequate power supply for lights.

Timelines and Meetings

Develop timelines to chart the progress of each committee function and be sure your committee chairs hold regular meetings. Every detail should be checked and double-checked. As the event draws near, the pace of activity will increase.

"Develop timelines to chart the progress of each committee function and be sure your committee chairs hold regular meetings."

Follow-up

After the event is over, make sure you return any equipment you may have borrowed and leave the site as you found it. After you've thanked your volunteers, get to work on their evaluations. While other staff members and volunteers collapse from exhaustion, a separate subcommittee should be working on ways to capitalize on interest in the organization generated by the event.

"After the event is over, make sure you return any equipment you may have borrowed and leave the site as you found it."

SAMPLE PLANS FOR AN AWARDS DINNER

An environmental education group decides to hold an event in mid- to late March to honor community leaders for their contributions to environmental causes. All proceeds from the event will benefit the organization. Planning for the event should begin no less than six months prior to the month it will be staged.

Sept. Determine the overall theme for the event. Set a tentative date. Meet with key staff people and volunteers to discuss a general outline of the evening. Recruit chairpeople and committee coordinators.

Oct. Appoint a site selection committee. Visit possible sites. Set a date. Select a site and make the necessary arrangements to reserve it. Determine your costs and create a budget.

Nov. Name committee chairpeople. Recruit committee members.

Committee responsible for invitations should develop a mailing list.

Program committee should contact and interview keynote speakers and emcees.

Menu committee should meet with hotel liaison or caterers.

Publicity committee should send out advance news release on the people involved.

Finance committee should organize the income and expense bookkeeping.

Decorations and equipment committee should develop decor incorporating the theme of the event.

Dec. **Invitation committee** produces and mails out invitations, holds date cards.

Jan. **Program committee** arranges additional entertainment, begins work on the program.

Menu committee determines the menu.

Publicity committee develops promotional material on the event.

Decorations committee assembles the decorations, visuals, etc.

Feb. **Invitation committee** records initial response, creates seating chart, follows up with individuals who have not responded.

Program committee confirms additional entertainment, solicits advertising for program, sends program to printer, arranges for specific awards.

Publicity committee places promotional material on event in media.

Mar. 3 Committee heads meet to review final plans.

Mar. 10 **Invitation committee** continues follow-up.

Program committee completes seating chart, approves final program scenario.

Menu committee confirms menu, estimates number of dinners.

Publicity committee provides media advisory and release on event.

Decorations committee assembles needed materials.

Mar. 17 **Program committee** makes final adjustments to program.

Menu committee confirms number of meals.

Publicity committee follows up on news release/media advisory.

Finance committee arranges for petty cash at event.

Decorations committee begins on-site set-up.

Mar. 18 Set-up completed. Dinner.

Mar. 19 **Finance committee** figures total income.

Decorations committee breaks down decorations, returns rented/borrowed equipment.

Mar. 21 **Invitation committee** sends thank-you notes to all committee members.

Program committee sends thank-you notes to reporters and broadcasters, reports income generated.

Finance committee pays bills.

Mar. 26 **Invitation committee** reviews list of attendees for future follow-up, updates all mailing lists.

All committee chairpeople meet to consider next year's dinner.

This checklist may help your various committees cover the key details:

Site Selection

- ☐ physical layout and general location
- ☐ traffic patterns
- ☐ availability of electricity, restrooms
- ☐ furniture/equipment needed
- ☐ other events scheduled in adjoining spaces
- ☐ police clearances/parking/security

Invitations

- ☐ preparation of mailing lists
- ☐ invitations and envelope addressing
- ☐ return cards and envelopes
- ☐ tickets or reservation cards
- ☐ printing
- ☐ postage
- ☐ card file to track responses and record information
- ☐ receipts for contributions or reservations received

Program

- ☐ invite speakers
- ☐ working agenda
- ☐ print program for the event
- ☐ souvenir program (an excellent way to produce additional income)
- ☐ make copies of speeches
- ☐ award certificates or plaques

☐ seating charts, name cards, place cards
☐ film and slides
☐ records and tapes
☐ displays and exhibits

Equipment

☐ banners, logos, signs
☐ decorations, centerpieces
☐ dais, head table, podium
☐ display and exhibit equipment
☐ chairs, tables
☐ buses, cars, or other means of transportation
☐ merchandise (for fairs, auctions, bazaars)
☐ information handouts
☐ special lighting
☐ sound system
☐ audiovisual equipment
☐ electrical outlets
☐ phones and fax machine

Finance

☐ budget
☐ accounting journals
☐ invoice procedures
☐ petty cash
☐ bank deposit procedures
☐ special bank accounts
☐ disbursement vouchers or purchase orders
☐ cash boxes
☐ system of receipts

Publicity

- ☐ news releases
- ☐ media advisories
- ☐ special media invitations and other "comps"
- ☐ paid advertising
- ☐ public-service announcements
- ☐ posters
- ☐ window and counter cards
- ☐ bumper stickers and buttons

Clean-up

- ☐ post-event clean-up
- ☐ thank-you's to speakers, special guests
- ☐ thank-you's to volunteers
- ☐ thank-you's to other providers of free materials, equipment
- ☐ return equipment
- ☐ thank-you's to vendors and other suppliers

7 Crisis Management

You direct a well-known charity and your good works have been in the news. Your high-profile board of directors is headed by a noted community leader. You have recently launched a major fundraising campaign.

And then you learn that your chief financial officer may be embezzling funds. A criminal investigation is about to begin. The situation calls into question not only the credibility of the entire organization; it also has the potential to generate enormous negative publicity and scare off your donors.

What do you do?

The scenarios may vary, but crises have an unfortunate habit of cropping up when they're least expected, threatening the equilibrium, if not the very existence, of an organization. They can disrupt routine activities, demoralize staff and volunteers, and erode your support in the community. Inevitably, they consume valuable time, energy, and resources.

But while you may not be able to avoid them, they *can* be managed.

The best way to deal with a crisis is to plan for it before it happens. Every organization, regardless of its size or budget, should have in place a *crisis committee* whose functions in the event of a crisis are to act as a "voice" for the organization; to deal with various constituents and stakeholders, including the board of directors, staff, volunteers, and major

"When a crisis breaks, it is the [crisis] committee's job to implement the organization's predetermined procedures . . . immediately.

donors; and to set policy and procedures. This committee should include the following:

- the organization's chief executive officer
- legal counsel
- the organization's public relations director
- outside public relations counsel, if retained
- the chairperson of the board, if appropriate

When a crisis breaks, it is the committee's job to implement the organization's predetermined procedures, or *crisis communications protocol*, immediately. The following outline of such a protocol is flexible enough to be adapted for use by almost any organization, large or small.

CRISIS COMMUNICATIONS PROTOCOL

1. *Determine the gravity of the situation.* Weigh the possible consequences and establish strategies to deal with them: What would be the results of negative media coverage? Reduced donor support? Damage to the organization's credibility? Is there a chance of a civil suit or criminal investigation? Attempt to determine the credibility of the reporter who uncovered the story as well as whether there is any way to keep it from being broken. Determine to what extent the crisis will interfere with normal business and, if appropriate, what needs to be done to make sure operations and/or services continue to run smoothly.

2. *Before the story breaks, develop position statements, answers to potential questions, and fact sheets that aggressively set forth your organization's position.* Gather and confirm all relevant facts and develop a basic statement that is short and to the point. Make sure that all statements are cleared with legal counsel and reviewed by public relations counsel.

Hold your position materials in reserve to use when and if they are needed. When and how you go public will depend on the crisis. In certain situations, an organization may want to hold its cards until forced to play them by questions from the media. In other situations, an organization may find it advantageous to be "out front" in a potentially damaging situation—making the news, in other words, rather than reacting to it.

3. *Notify your major stakeholders.* Your board of directors should be notified and asked for its input as early as possible. At the very least, make sure your board learns about the crisis from you and not from a reporter. Similarly, notify your major benefactors as soon as possible. Finally, make sure that key staff are notified—how and when will depend on the situation.

Assemble a list of "friends" who should receive a copy of your basic statement and any other special mailings you do in response to the situation. These friends should be credible supporters of the organization and, to the extent possible, should be kept on standby to speak on its behalf.

If statements or other materials are to be circulated widely, distribute them at the same time—*and prior to the appearance of a story*, if possible. Generally speaking, communications in a crisis situation should be direct and coordinated so that your various stakeholders are informed at the same time.

4. *Direct all media inquiries to a single spokesperson.* In selecting a spokesperson, keep in mind that he or she should be your organization's *only* voice as the situation unfolds. Your spokesperson should understand the media and know how to deal with reporters, and he or she should have the time to handle the situation effectively.

When dealing with reporters, a spokesperson should follow these guidelines:

". . . communications in a crisis situation should be direct and coordinated so that your various stakeholders are informed at the same time."

"Assume that all interviews are on the record."

- Never refuse to talk to a reporter; to do so is to relinquish control of the story.
- Make it your business to know reporters' deadlines and return their calls so that they can make those deadlines.
- Decide on the key points you need to get across and, no matter what the questions, make these points during the interview.
- Ascertain what reporters know *before* answering any questions. This can be done by simply asking a reporter what the nature of the story is and what he or she has learned so far. By assessing the extent of the reporter's knowledge, you'll be in a better position to decide how much additional information to give out.
- Assume that all interviews are on the record. If you want to make a statement off the record, you must say so *before* you make the statement, not after, and keep in mind that facts made off the record may be attributed to an "anonymous source."
- If you don't understand a question, say so.
- If you don't know the answer to a question, say so and offer to call the reporter back with the answer.
- Offer to give the reporter the names of other sources who might provide third-party endorsements of your organization.
- If a reporter is hostile and you don't want to answer a question, simply answer yes or no. *DON'T ELABORATE AND DON'T EXPLAIN!*
- Ask when the story will appear.

5. *Follow crisis procedures.* Update the crisis committee on a regular basis. Take stock of new developments and review media coverage daily. Assess whether and/or when a statement or fact

sheet needs to be revised to reflect new developments. Continue to update stakeholders and meet with staff as needed.

6. *Conduct follow-up after the crisis has been resolved.* Touch base with all interested parties and bring them up to date. If the crisis involved an organizational problem that was corrected, make sure news of the solution is circulated. And finally, thank everyone who helped you handle the situation effectively.

8 The New Communications Technologies

"A new Information Age is dawning, and it will be as total a break with the past as the one Gutenberg helped spawn in the 1400s."
—*TV Guide*

New advances in communications, including the development of personal computers, facsimile machines, cellular phones, and the proliferation of computer networks comprising the early stages of the so-called "information superhighway," have significant implications for the public relations or communications professional.

This chapter will outline some of the ways in which these changes are having an effect on the work and effectiveness of communicators. Much of what follows, however, will be subject to further revision in a short period of time. In order to keep abreast of the new communications technologies, it's necessary to read everything you can get your hands on—not only newspapers and consumer magazines but trade journals and the advertising that appears in them. In fact, advertisements are often the best place to learn about the development and availability of new technologies adapted for communications.

"When considering the many possibilities of the new technologies, don't forget that technology exists to serve the user, not the other way around."

OFFICE COMMMUNICATIONS

Personal computers and related digital technologies such as the fax and networked communications applications have made it easier for non-profit organizations to compete with for-profit businesses. The price of microprocessors and computer workstations continues to drop, while the benefits of having a high-end machine continue to accrue. For instance, instead of having to stand by a fax machine for hours feeding in page after page, by installing a fax board on your personal computer you can send faxes to hundreds of people simultaneously in a matter of minutes.

When considering the many possibilities of the new technologies, don't forget that technology exists to serve the user, not the other way around. Just as "technophobia" may prevent some people from joining the computer age, others may indulge in technological overkill, purchasing hardware and software that's far too complicated—and expensive—for the tasks at hand. With a little research and experimentation, most organizations can find a happy medium between these extremes that will make their staffs more productive and save them time and money

Media List Manipulation

Computers have changed the way organizations communicate with the media. At the most basic level, a good word-processing application can store thousands of names and addresses and print labels and envelopes at a moment's notice. The same kind of software also makes it easier to personalize cover letters, pitch letters, and other promotional materials created for mass distribution.

However, the greatest potential for computerized management of media lists lies not with word-processing applications but with other kinds of software. Whether you are sending information tailored to reporters on certain beats, updating a list of newsletter subscribers, or trying to figure out why a certain letter keeps coming back marked "Return to Sender," a media list requires constant pruning and reseeding. A good database program can make these chores simpler.

Database programs generally are written so that mailing lists can be entered into the computer with a variety of qualifying information in addition to the contact's name, affiliation, and address. Additional *fields*, or categories of information, you might want to have in your database include the contact's beat, what kind of medium he or she works in (print or broadcast), broadcast or publication frequency, the type of audience targeted (trade or consumer), the geographic focus of the publication or broadcast (national, regional, local), the political orientation of the publication or broadcast (if any), and so on. The list can then be sorted and re-sorted so that each mailing is targeted to a carefully defined set of contacts according to the story being pitched.

Similar software is available for fundraising purposes. Contacts can be coded according to event, amount contributed, and so on. This not only allows an organization to target fundraising prospects for a specific event, it can also help in projecting the outcome of a fundraising event or campaign. (See the appendix for a list of organizations that assist nonprofits in choosing appropriate software applications.)

Printing Technologies/Desktop Publishing

Desktop-publishing software allows even inexperienced computer users to produce high-quality newsletters, invitations and RSVP cards, brochures, and other promotional materials for a fraction of the cost a professional printer would charge. For as little as $2,000 you can buy all the hardware—a standard PC and a laserjet printer—you'll need. The cost of basic graphics and desktop-publishing software usually runs from $150 to $500. With a little practice, the time and money you save producing these materials in-house can be considerable.

THE INFORMATION SUPERHIGHWAY

The idea of an "information superhighway" has generated an enormous amount of discussion about the future of communications in the 21st century. In the minds of many critics and commentators, the "information superhighway" is already here in the form of the Internet, a vast worldwide assemblage of some 15,000 computer networks. As most of its devotees know, the "Net" evolved from a Defense Department experiment in computer networking nearly 25 years ago and was designed to survive a nuclear war. Should one of its *nodes*, or central relay points, be knocked out in such a war, whatever was left of the network would continue to function—or that was the idea. Over the years, the upgrading and maintenance of the original infrastructure devolved onto the National Science Foundation and various civilian institutions, chiefly universities. Computer enthusiasts followed. Today, it's estimated that some 15 million computer users in this country alone navigate the Internet on a regular basis, and if usage continues to grow at its current rate, every computer user on the planet will be using the Net by the year 2000.

Getting access to the Internet requires three basic tools: a computer, a modem, and a subscription to a commercial online service or a relationship with an access provider. *Modems* are devices that allow information to be transferred from one computer to another via telephone lines. They

"Today, it's estimated that some 15 million computer users in this country alone navigate the Internet on a regular basis. . . ."

do this by translating the digitized information that all computers traffic in into signals that can be transmitted over phone lines to another computer with a modem, which translates the signal back into a digital stream that can be processed by the receiving computer.

In addition to being essential for gaining access to the Internet, modems can be used for a variety of basic tasks, such as transmitting a word-processed document from a main office in New York to a branch office in Chicago, where it can be printed out in a matter of minutes. As with regular phone calls, the cost of sending digitized information via a modem is determined by the amount of time it takes to send that information; the smaller the file and faster the transmission, the cheaper the cost—in many instances, cheaper than overnight mail service. Sending information this way also has advantages over facsimile transmissions, in that documents received as digital files can be readily converted into text and edited. And because hard copy can be generated by a letter-quality printer at the receiving end, the appearance of documents is superior—an important consideration when transmitting proposals and reports.

"Sending information this way also has advantages over facsimile transmissions, in that documents received as digital files can be readily converted into text and edited."

Once you've installed a modem, the two most popular ways to access the Internet are through a commercial online service such as CompuServe, America Online, or Prodigy, or through an access provider. Typically, both online services and access providers charge their customers a basic monthly fee (much like a cable company) for limited use of their Internet connections; additional time spent online results in extra charges. (InterNic, a group run by the National Science Foundation, provides a free listing of access providers; call 1-800-444-4345.)

What are the benefits of Internet access for nonprofit organizations? The most popular uses of the Net include electronic mail, access to a mind-expanding range of information stored in databases at universities and government bureaus around the world, and participating in online conferences and information-sharing with other nonprofit organizations.

The World Wide Web

Amid all the hype, the most talked about aspect of the Internet is the World Wide Web (WWW), or "Web." The Web uses a computer programming language called Hypertext Markup Language, or HTML, to organize and transmit digitized text, graphic, audio, and (with the right software) full-motion video files over the Internet. For your computer to properly interpret files encoded in HTML, however, you need a software application called a *browser.* All the major commercial online services mentioned above now provide Web access and their own browsers as part of their services. If you decide to go with an access provider instead of an online service, Compuserve's "Internet in a Box" package includes browser software, or you can buy or download the very popular browser offered by the Netscape Corporation (http://www.netscape.com).

For nonprofit organizations, the advantages to establishing a presence, or "site," on the Web are many. In general, the communitarian ethos of the Internet makes it an ideal vehicle for nonprofits to share their ideas and resources. And unlike a brochure or video, Web sites can contain an almost limitless amount of information and can be updated as often as needed. (Indeed any information you put on the Web *should* be updated at least monthly, so that visitors to your site will be encouraged to come back.)

As interest in the Web continues to grow, the tools for building a Web site are becoming more accessible to computer neophytes. There are dozens of "how-to" manuals available in bookstores, and the same kind of information is readily available online—at no cost. For the less adventurous, software applications that translate text into HTML and help you create graphics for your site can be purchased for a few hundred dollars. A number of the commercial online services also allow you to create (for a fee) your own *home page* with a limited amount of information. At the opposite end of the spectrum, you can hire a company that specializes in Web design to construct and maintain a site for your organization. Prices generally start at $10,000, with the minimum monthly maintenance charge running anywhere from $200-$1,000.

Once your nonprofit has established a site on the Web, take a look at the services offered by an umbrella organization such as the Institute for Global Communications (http://www.igc.apc.org/igc/igcinfo.html). IGC is the U.S. member of the Association for Progressive Communications, an international coalition of computer networks that provides tools for information exchange to more than 20,000 activists and nonprofit organizations in some 94 countries. The IGC networks include PeaceNet (human rights and social justice advocacy); EcoNet (environmental preservation and sustainability); ConflictNet (social justice and conflict resolution); LaborNet (economic justice and workers' rights); and WomensNet (women's resources and computer networking). Subscribing to any one of these networks gives users full access to all IGC networks, including a direct link to the Internet and World Wide Web. IGC wil also help nonprofit groups establish their Web sites.

How can one of these networks help a small nonprofit group? Using PeaceNet, a New York City-based human rights monitoring group recently downloaded the entire text of the U.S. Department of State's report on human rights abuses around the world just two days after it was published. Many other government departments and bureaus are starting to make their documents available online as well. For example, through the Internet, interested parties can gain access to California's daily legislative calendar, a roster of its senate and assembly members, the text of bills passed and pending, and the text of the state constitution.

". . . Web sites can contain an almost limitless amount of information and can be updated as often as needed."

VIDEO TECHNOLOGIES

CD-ROM

When upgrading your office computer systems, it may be worthwhile to add CD-ROM capability. The same size and shape as regular compact discs, CD-ROM discs cannot be recorded over (hence the ROM, for "read-only memory"). In addition to sound, they hold pictures, video, and text—about 400 times the data that can fit on a typical floppy disk. Books, catalogues, encyclopedias, and numerous commercial publications are now available on CD-ROM, and more can be expected in the next five years. Research tools such as LEXIS/NEXIS, media databases, and clipping services—even the telephone directories for an entire state—can be accessed and updated via CD-ROM. More and more newsrooms are adding CD-ROM to their systems as well. According to a recent Associated Press survey, 600 out of 1,000 newspapers are using CD-ROM equipment, allowing them to download publicity photos via modem from anywhere in the world.

Videotape and Video News Releases

One of the most common uses of video by communications professionals is the *video news release* (VNR). This is a videotaped news segment, three to five minutes in length, produced by publicists to blend in with the look and style of professional news broadcasts. It is then mass-distributed to news directors around the country for incorporation into local news programs. VNRs often result in significant prime-time television coverage. And, because they are organization-produced, they provide much greater control over the message delivered than a station-produced story.

The principal drawback to VNRs lies in the fact that news directors of larger stations often dismiss them automatically. A basic rule of thumb is that the smaller the station, the more likely it will be to use a VNR. The reason is simple. Smaller stations have smaller production budgets and fewer camera crews; thus, they're more likely to utilize a news segment supplied to them free of charge.

Despite the fact that they are used infrequently by big stations, effective VNRs are capable of reaching audiences totaling in the millions. What makes a VNR effective? Good production values, for starters. The temptation to spend a few thousand dollars on video equipment and produce a video in-house may be great, but yielding to the temptation can be foolish. Newsrooms are looking for network-quality production values, and a story that is crafted by an experienced hand at broadcast journalism is more likely to exhibit those values. A frequent objection of news producers to the use of these "canned" segments is that they tend to be biased or commercial. A release that looks as much like station-produced news segments as possible stands the greatest chance of being aired.

Flexibility is also an important factor, since it encourages VNR use by facilitating customization. For example, the news announcer at a local station can do the voiceover for a VNR, provided a script is sent with the tape. Extra footage and *sound bites* allow for custom editing, so the station can make the segment unique. It can even add a local angle. Think about how the story would work as a 30-second spot, a 90-second spot, a five-minute piece, and so on.

VNRs can be produced at an average cost of $12,000 to $14,000, but may cost as much as $50,000 depending on a variety of factors, including the number of shooting locations and the production timetable (a fast-breaking story can entail overtime fees). Distribution costs can add from $500 to $5,000. The lower figure is for a one-time simultaneous satellite feed to hundreds of stations; the higher figure is for the duplication and mailing of 200 videocassettes.

A third alternative is to mass-mail scripts and storyboards—cartoon-like renderings of the segment sketched in a few frames—to news directors along with a self-addressed, stamped postcard to be used to order a copy of the tape. This way, costs are accrued only for the duplication of videocassettes that have been requested and have a good chance of being aired.

The cost of VNRs may come down as new desktop publishing technologies are applied to video production. Videos shot on digitized film can be edited and produced on a desktop computer and sent by modem to news producers, saving money on packaging and shipping costs. Many video production studios have updated their facilities with this type of system, which may translate into lower production and distribution costs to your organization. It pays to shop around and ask questions.

Companies that specialize in soup-to-nuts production and satellite distribution of VNRs will direct, produce, and distribute VNRs via satellite to TV stations and news outlets across the country.

While VNRs may be the most common communications use of video, there are other uses as well. The applications of videotape are limited only by the imagination and run the gamut from the creation of public-service announcements for local TV stations to full-scale documentaries to be aired on public television or public-access cable channels. And because they provide a break from the proverbial talking-heads format, organizational videos are often used whenever a spokesperson appears on a news interview program.

In addition to their use in large-scale publicity campaigns, informational videotapes can also be prepared for small, specialized audiences—meetings of an organization's members; directors, or potential funders,

"The cost of VNRs may come down as new desktop publishing technologies are applied to video production."

for example. Many performing arts groups have found this an effective means of "auditioning" before grantmakers, and such tapes have also found their way into public education programs, special events, and the like.

Private-use tapes need not be produced to the standards required for broadcast distribution, and therefore may be considerably less expensive. Video equipment can be acquired, or crews rented, for relatively little, and its accessibility has made the video camera a common presence at all sorts of organizational events, from conferences to award ceremonies.

PSAs

As a less expensive alternative to VNRs, public-service announcements (PSAs) can spread your organization's message, often using existing footage, celebrity or institutional spokespersons, and so on.

Some satellite distribution services, such as Potomac Television/Communications in Washington, D.C., offer PSA distribution free of charge through its PSA Channel, which reaches more than 700 television stations around the country via satellite. The convenience the service offers to PSA directors enhances a tape's chance of getting on the air. Instead of loading and unloading dozens of tapes, directors can downlink a satellite feed in their preferred video format, review the spots, and select any number of PSAs for programming. This service is ideal for smaller organizations and nonprofits that cannot afford the expense of a national mailing and follow-up distribution. For an additional non-negotiable fee, the company will provide a usage report to nonprofits.

SATELLITE MEDIA TOURS/VIDEO NEWS CONFERENCES

The Satellite Media Tour

Not too long ago, a grassroots organization faced a critical juncture after years of issue campaigning. A crucial piece of legislation the group had worked years to introduce was being debated in Congress, and the President had promised to sign the bill if enacted. The group needed to reach key constituents and legislators in targeted media markets, but it didn't have the resources or time to send a spokesperson from city to city with its message. Instead, a satellite media tour brought its spokesperson to every key city it targeted without that person ever leaving Washington, D.C.

This is still another example of the ways in which technology is revolutionizing the communications industry. The satellite media tour (SMT) saves your organization's spokesperson from the rigors of an "If this is Tuesday, it must be Toledo" travel schedule. Instead, he or she can sit in a local studio and be interviewed by as many as five talk show hosts in the space of an hour.

Essentially, the satellite media tour is a controlled interview between a news station and the organization's spokesperson. While the video image of the spokesperson is beamed out via satellite, the spokesperson, sitting in a studio, wears a fitted earpiece that transmits questions from the reporter via a special telephone line called Interruptable Fold Back (IFB). Typically, the interviews are broken down into five-minute blocks, with five interviews per half-hour, allowing a minute or so between interviews to get the next station ready. The result is something akin to the interviews usually seen on ABC's "Nightline" or PBS' "NewsHour with Jim Lehrer."

The advantages of a satellite media tour over a more customary media tour are the savings in a spokesperson's time and an organization's money. SMTs are also a great way to reach the geographic area most important to an organization. For instance, the National Committee to Preserve Social Security and Medicare, a leading senior advocacy group, targets its SMTs directly to stations in the Sunbelt.

According to an on-air business anchor at a TV station in Detroit, "Satellite media tours enable us to get in touch with key people at a really low cost. They let me know first-hand which angle an organization is going to take on certain issues."

Satellite interviews can have a tremendous impact on a station's audience. This impact can be increased by providing additional visual information. For instance, a satellite interview can be conducted in conjunction with a video news release. If a fully produced VNR is not financially feasible, then consider transmitting video footage, or a b-roll, that a station can incorporate into its own news stories. The additional video can be distributed before, after, or between interviews.

Costs for a satellite media tour can run as low as $7,000, with an organization's public relations department handling the placement. Potomac Television, mentiomed above, offers *turnkey tours*, including placement, technical and production arrangements, and evaluation, with the cost averaging roughly $11,000 for an hour-long tour.

Video News Conferences

A video news conference has several advantages over the traditional news conference. Organizations not based in a major media market such as New York City, Washington, D.C., or Los Angeles but with an

> *"The advantages of a satellite media tour over a more customary media tour are the savings in a spokesperson's time and an organization's money."*

announcement of national import to make can use a video news conference to communicate simultaneously with media representatives in those markets. A conference site is arranged in each selected city (possibilities include the approximately 300 public television stations linked by satellite and national hotel and motel chains with conference facilities), and telephone hookups allow reporters at selected sites and other audience members to ask questions and watch the responses on closed-circuit television.

As with the satellite media tour, travel costs are reduced when there is a need to have the participation of large numbers of geographically scattered groups or individuals. Via satellite, they can attend without ever having to leave their hometown or city. The approach is superior to telephone interviews, since it allows for more spontaneity, interpersonal contacts, and the use of visuals at the originating site.

The drama, as well as the novelty, of a telepress conference might be enough to attract media attention. However, depending on the facilities involved, the number of interconnects, the amount of satellite time required, whether all sites will have video or telephone interconnects (that is, cameras in each site or only telephone receivers), and other factors, the costs can vary greatly. For major national or regional announcements or meetings, the concept is certainly worth exploring.

9 Evaluating a Public Relations Effort

After all the explanations and advice, it seems appropriate to close this book with an examination of the methods that can help you evaluate your public relations programs and techniques.

Unfortunately, the art of public relations is difficult to quantify. Unlike advertising or fundraising, the response generated by your efforts is not necessarily measured by how many purchases have been made or how many dollars have been raised. Rather, public relations success must be measured by assessing attitudinal changes, be it greater credibility accorded an organization in the media or increased public support for an issue. One of the key tools for measuring these types of changes is a public relations plan with clearly defined objectives. At a minimum, it is the only way an organization can determine whether its planned activities worked—and worked well—and whether key audiences were reached.

Beyond the public relations plan, there are a number of services that have developed tools which, to the extent possible, help the public relations practitioner quantify results. The services these companies provide range from a simple calculation of "impressions" generated by a clip (calculated at 2.5 times circulation) to companies that generate detailed analyses of where and when your message appeared and whether or not those "appearances" communicated what you wanted to say. (If you plan

". . . evaluation works best when it's done on a regular basis."

to use this kind of service, be sure to speak with a representative of the company to determine whether your goals are measurable.)

Remember, evaluation works best when it's done on a regular basis. Many organizations will be well served by an evaluation program that measures results at least twice a year. This kind of proactive approach does a better job of letting you know when your communications program isn't working or has gone astray. Similarly, if your budget permits, an ideal way to begin an evaluation program is to identify important issues and organizational attitudes with a benchmarking study prior to the start of the program.

The following is a partial list of public relations services (see pages 174–175 for a more complete list):

- *Luce Press Clippings*—Provides the basic clipping service plus a count of impressions, circulations, and advertising equivalencies.

- *News Analysis Institute*—An example of the second tier of measurement: NAI will review the placement of your messages from a regional perspective and offer a slightly more in-depth analysis of your results as well as the number of impressions.

- *Copernicus*—Will develop an analysis of your program results, keying into your objectives, audiences reached, market penetration, etc., as well as provide the basic clipping counts.

- *The Delahaye Group*—Probably the most sophisticated of all measurement companies. Delahaye delves deeply into the qualitative and the quantitative aspects of your program, providing reports on competitive perspectives, market analyses, message analysis, etc., as well as the clipping information. Will also supply charts and graphs if that's important to you when presenting results to management and your board of directors.

If you're not able to engage a service to evaluate your public relations results, there are a number of other techniques to evaluate program effectiveness.

1. *An analysis of inquiries.* Keep records of mail and telephone calls from the general public and from your members. Listen to what they're saying. Are they contacting you

more often? Is their response different (better?) than a year ago?

2. *Publicity.* Keep track of coverage by the media over a period of time. What are members of the media saying about you? What are they covering? What are they avoiding? What are they criticizing and what are they lauding? Are you receiving too little coverage or too much? How does the public react to coverage of your organization by the media? Who is covering you? Who isn't? Why? Who are they covering instead? Why?

3. *A survey of management perceptions.* What messages do management and the board want to see communicated? What public relations problems do they perceive?

4. *A budget analysis.* Examine how your organization's budget has evolved, as well as how the public relations component of that budget has been developed. What is the budget planning cycle? How have your priorities shifted over the years and how are new priorities reflected in the budget? Reexamine your public relations plan and goals.

5. *A materials review.* Review the materials your organization has created, including brochures, news releases, annual reports, newsletters, direct-mail pieces, advertisements, posters, and fundraising literature. Who gets them? How much does each cost? Do they duplicate other materials? How effective are they? Is a single department responsible for coordinating their development, design, and distribution? Do you have a distribution and development plan?

6. *Outside counsel.* Hire outside public relations counsel for an objective examination of your public relations needs and programs. In addition to reviewing your materials, an outside firm can ask media representatives, important civic leaders, and other individuals about the strengths and weaknesses in your public relations work.

7. *Audience analysis.* Set up a checklist of all the groups you are currently reaching. Rate your organization on how well you are communicating with each group. This will force you to take a hard, objective look at where you are. It also will help you begin the process of identifying your potential audiences and provide a basis for later evaluation.

8. *Crisis management.* If there has been a crisis, how strong was your public relations response? Were you able to move

> *"What are members of the media saying about you? . . . Are you receiving too little coverage or too much?"*

swiftly and effectively? If not, how can you alter your plans
to produce better results next time?

9. *Self-assessment.* Plan a retreat (some optimists call it an
"advance") for a staff discussion of these questions. Examine the results of this session.

A full evaluation should lead naturally into developing next year's
public relations effort. The evaluation might include a public relations
audit or merely a realignment of objectives, audiences, and strategies as
discussed. At its very best, public relations is a tool for self-examination,
the eternal ombudsperson for what is true and real, and the sounding
board for what is credible.

Appendix A

Public Relations Resources and Commercial Services

PRINT PUBLICITY RESOURCES

Bacon's Newspaper and Magazine Directories are annual directories that provide data on media contacts for more than 24,000 U.S. and Canadian newspapers and 10,000 magazines, arranged into approximately 100 categories. Published by Bacon's Information Inc., 332 South Michigan Avenue, Chicago, Illinois 60604. Tel: (800) 621-0561, ext. 4502; Fax: (312) 922-3127.

Broadcasting & Cable Yearbook provides information about radio stations, television stations, and cable outlets in the United States and Canada. Published by Reed Reference, 121 Chanlon Road, New Providence, New Jersey 07974. Tel: (908) 464-6800; Fax: (908) 771-7704.

College Media Directory is an annual directory that lists more than 6,000 periodicals published by students. Published by Oxbridge Communications, 150 Fifth Avenue, Suite 302, New York,

New York 10011. Tel: (212) 741-0231; Fax: (212) 633-2938; e-mail: fshapiro@oxbridge.com.

CONTACTS is a weekly newsletter listing publicity opportunities for various media outlets. Each week a different subject/topic (e.g., personal finance, travel, holidays) is highlighted. A brief description of each outlet, its interests, and requirements follows. Includes personnel changes. Published by MerComm, Inc., 75 S. Highland Ave., Ossining, New York 10562. Tel: (914) 923-9400; Fax: (914) 923-9484; e-mail: contactpr@aol.com.

Editor & Publisher International Yearbook is the most complete and authentic record of the newspaper business. Also available on CD-ROM. Published by Editor & Publisher Company, 11 West 19th Street, New York, New York 10011. Tel: (212) 675-4380; Fax: (212) 691-6939.

Jack O'Dwyer's Newsletter is a weekly newsletter that reports information and news related to the public relations industry. Published by J.R. O'Dwyer Co., 271 Madison Avenue, New York, New York 10016. Tel: (212) 679-2471; Fax: (212) 683-2750.

Gebbie Press All-In-One Directory contains listings of daily and weekly newspapers, radio and television stations, news magazines, and trade press publications. Published by Gebbie Press, P.O. Box 1000, New Paltz, New York 12561. Tel: (212) 255-7560.

Hudson's Washington News Media Contacts Directory contains extensive data for more than 5,000 publications, wire services, bureaus, correspondents, editors, and freelance writers in the D.C. area. Published by Howard Penn Hudson, P.O. Box 311, Rhinebeck, New York 12572. Also publishes **Hudson's State Capitals News Media Contacts** and **Hudson's Subscription Newsletter Directories.** Tel: (914) 876-2081; Fax: (914) 876-2561; e-mail: HPHudson@aol.com.

New York Publicity Outlets includes information on the New York metropolitan and tri-state area (New York, New Jersey, Connecticut), daily and weekly newspapers, consumer magazines (based in or covering the area), radio and television stations, interview programs, trade publications, and syndicates. Also publishes **Metro California Media Directory.** Public Relations Plus, Inc., Box 1197, New Milford, Connecticut 06776. Tel: (203) 354-9361; Fax: (800) 588-3827; e-mail: 74044.3050@compuserve.com.

News Media Yellow Book is published quarterly and lists names, addresses, and telephone numbers of reporters, writers, editors, and producers in the national news media. Published by Monitor Leadership Directories, Inc., 104 Fifth Avenue, New York, New York 10011. Tel: (212) 627-4140; Fax: (212) 627-1612/1709.

Oxbridge Directory of Newsletters lists more than 20,000 newsletters arranged into approximately 260 categories. Published by Oxbridge Communications, Inc., 150 Fifth Avenue, Suite 302, New York, New York 10011. Tel: (212) 741-0231; Fax: (212) 633-2938; e-mail: fshapiro@oxbridge.com.

PARTYLINE is a weekly newsletter that lists media placement opportunities and personnel changes. Published by Morton Yarmon, 35 Sutton Place, New York, New York 10022. Tel: (212) 755-3487; Fax: (212) 755-3488; e-mail: byarmon@ix.netcom.com.

The Working Press of the Nation consists of four volumes covering more than 200,000 print and broadcast media contacts, feature writers, and photographers. Published by Reed Reference Publishing, 121 Chanlon Road, New Providence, New Jersey 07974. Tel: (908) 464-6800; Fax: (908) 464-3553/3645.

BROADCAST PUBLICITY RESOURCES

Bacon's TV/Cable and Radio Directories are annual directories that provide data on media contacts at more than 10,000 radio stations, 1,200 television stations, and 800 cable outlets. Published by Bacon's Information Inc., 332 South Michigan Avenue, Chicago, Illinois 60604. Tel: (800) 621-0561; Fax: (312) 922-3127.

Broadcasting Yearbook lists radio and television stations, their markets, network affiliations, and broadcast reach. Published by Reed Reference Book Publishing, 121 Chanlon Road, New Providence, New Jersey 07974. Tel: (800) 521-8110.

Handbook of Information for United States Public Television contains personnel listings for educational television and Public Broadcasting Service affiliate stations. Published by the Corporation for Public Broadcasting, 901 E Street, N.W., Washington, D.C. 20004. Tel: (202) 879-9764; Fax: (202) 783-1019; e-mail: rschooley@cpb.org.

Radio–TV Contact Service lists New York local and network radio and television contacts. The service is provided by Television Index, 40-29 27th Street, Long Island City, New York 11101. Tel: (718) 937-3990; Fax: (718) 937-5432.

COMMERCIAL PUBLIC RELATIONS SERVICES

Associated Release Service distributes short features and columns to newspapers (mostly weeklies) nationally. Editors often use this material as filler. Associated Release Service, 43 North Canal Street, Chicago, Illinois 60606. Tel: (312) 726-8693; Fax: (312) 726-8596.

Burrelle's tracks publicity about your organization in newspapers around the country. A clipping service is particularly useful in tracking items that local chapters might generate. Most clipping services charge a monthly fee, plus a handling charge for each clipping forwarded to the client. Burrelle's, 75 East Northfield Avenue, Livingston, NJ 07039. Tel: (800) 631-1160; Fax: (201) 992-7675/1736.

Copernicus provides basic clipping counts and can analyze your program results by objective, audiences reached, market penetration, and so on. Copernicus, 315 Post Road West, Westport, Connecticut 06880. Tel: (203) 221-7100; Fax: (203) 221-8465.

The Delahaye Group delves deeply into the qualitative and quantitative aspects of your public relations program, providing reports on competitive perspectives, market analyses, message analyses, clipping information, and much more. The Delahaye Group, Delahaye Wharf, 117 Bow Street, Portsmouth, New Hampshire 03801. Tel: (603) 431-0111; Fax: (603) 431-0669.

Derus Media Service prepares and distributes press releases, camera-ready photo features, and press kits to all media in the United States, Canada, and Latin America. Other services include Spanish-language translations and survey research. Derus Media Service, Inc., 500 N. Dearborn Street, Suite 516, Chicago, Illinois 60610. Tel: (312) 644-4360; Fax: (312) 644-9192.

Luce Press Clippings tracks publicity about your organization in newspapers around the country. A clipping service is particularly useful in tracking items that local chapters might generate. Most clipping services charge a monthly fee, plus a handling charge for each clipping forwarded to the client. Luce Press Clippings, 420 Lexington Avenue,

Suite 203, New York, New York 10017. Tel: (212) 889-6711; Fax: (212) 481-0105.

Luce Teleclip service provides transcripts and videotapes of network and local TV programs. Luce Press Clippings, 42 South Center, Mesa, Arizona 85210. Tel: (602) 834-4884; Fax: (602) 834-3821; e-mail: clip@lucepress.com; Web URL: http://www.lucepress.com/www/clip.

Media Distribution Service maintains media lists and will package and distribute press material. Media Distribution Service, 307 West 36th Street, New York, New York 10001. Tel: (212) 279-4800; Fax: (212) 714-9092.

Metro News Publicity Network maintains media lists and will package and distribute press material. Metro News Publicity Network, 33 West 34th Street, New York, New York 10001. Tel: (212) 947-5100; Fax: (212) 714-9139.

News Analysis Institute reviews the placement of your messages from a regional perspective and offers an in-depth analysis of the results as well as a count of the impressions. News Analysis Institute, 818 Liberty Avenue, Pittsburgh, Pennsylvania 15222. Tel: (412) 471-9411.

Nielsen Media Research tracks usages of video news releases, public service announcements, satellite media tours, and electronic press kits. Nielsen Media Research, 299 Park Avenue, New York, New York, 10171. Tel: (212) 708-7500; Fax: (212) 708-775; Web URL: http://www.nielsenmedia.com.

North American Precis Syndicate distributes short features and columns to newspapers (mostly weeklies) nationally. Editors often use this material as fillers. North American Precis Syndicate, 201 East 42nd Street, New York, New York 10017. Tel: (212) 867-9000; Fax: (212) 983-0970.

PR Newswire acts as a wire service for publicists. For a fee, it will distribute your story over the wire to subscribers. This service differs from the Associated Press and United Press International in that all stories submitted get carried. PR Newswire, 810 7th Avenue, 35th floor, New York, New York 10019. Tel: (212) 596-1500; Web URL: http://www.quote.com/info/prnews.html.

PTA Satellite provides a variety of services, including domestic and international satellite TV tours, video production, electronic press kits, b-roll news feeds, press junkets, video news releases, live media events, tele-conferences, and media training. PTA Satellite, 301 East 57th Street, 3rd Floor, New York, New York 10022. Tel: (212) 593-5820; Fax: (212) 715-1665; e-mail: ptActive@aol.com.

Quark Video provides standards conversion, production services, and duplication. Quark Video, 109 West 27th Street, New York, New York 10001. Tel: (212) 807-7711.

Radio-TV Reports monitors radio and television publicity about your organization. Transcripts and videotapes of network and local TV programs are available. Radio–TV Reports, Inc., 317 Madison Avenue, 4th floor, New York, New York 10017. Tel: (212) 309-1400; Fax: (212) 309-1439.

Worldwide Productions offers a variety of services, including video tele-conferencing, video new releases, video production services, video transmissions, satellite media tours, camera crews, film and video libraries, and program production. Worldwide Television New Productions, 1995 Broadway, 8th floor, New York, New York 10023.

Appendix B

Information Technology Resources and Services

Arts Wire is a national computer network providing a forum for information and exchange within the arts community. Arts Wire subscriptions include a connection to the Internet through the Meta Network. Arts Wire, 824 South Mill Avenue, Suite 93, Tempe, Arizona 85281-5603. Tel: (602) 829-0815; e-mail: artswire@artswire.org; Web URL: http://www.tmn.com/Oh/Artswire/www/awfront.html.

Bacon's Directory on Disk, a CD-ROM version of Bacon's media directories, covers all print and broadcast outlet plus their editorial contacts. Bacon's Information Inc., 332 South Michigan Avenue, Chicago, Illinois 60604. Tel: (800) 621-0561; Fax: (312) 922-3127.

Blackbaud offers a complete line of PC-based software systems/products for not-for-profit development and administration professionals. Blackbaud, 4401 Belle Oaks Drive, Charleston, South Carolina 29405. Tel: (803) 740-5400; Fax: (803) 740-5412.

The Computer Guide for Non-Profits is a special advertising supplement published annually in the February issue of *The Chronicle of Philanthropy*. Contains descriptions of fundraising and other software, with toll-free numbers for ordering information. The Chronicle of Philanthropy, 1255 23rd Street, N.W., Washington, D.C. 20037. Tel: (202) 466-1200; Fax: (202) 466-2078; e-mail: editor@chronicle.com.

DataTimes sends you information on your industry via fax, LAN, or PC. Computers scan newswires, articles, broadcast transcripts, company profiles, financial data, newspapers, magazines, and TV news shows. DataTimes, 14000 Quail Springs Parkway, Suite 450, Oklahoma City, OK 73134. Tel: (405) 751-6400; Fax: (405) 755-8028.

Education Center for Community Organizing (ECCO) co-sponsors an annual conference on Computers for Social Change, which includes workshops, demonstrations, technical assistance, affinity groups, and a resource room. ECCO, Hunter College School of Social Work, 129 East 79th Street, New York, New York 10021. Tel: (212) 452-7112.

Institute for Global Communications provides computer networking tools for international communication and information exchange, including PeaceNet, EcoNet, ConflictNet, and LaborNet. Subscribing to any one of these networks gives you full access to all IGC networks. IGC is also a point of access for the Usenet system of inter-university bulletin boards. U.S. member, Association for Progressive Communications. Institute for Global Communications, 18 De Boom Street, San Francisco, California 94107. Tel: (415) 442-0220; Fax: (415) 546-1794; e-mail: subscription@igc.apc.org; Web URL: http://www.igc.apc.org/igc/services.html.

SpinControl II features a database compiled by Burrelle's that contains press contacts at most broadcast and print media outlets. It also offers contact management, targeted press release distribution, letter and mail label generation, and high-volume broadcast faxing. SPINWARE, Software Publishing, Inc., 12960 SW 133 Court, Miami, Florida 33186. Tel: (305) 254-5664; Fax: (305) 254-4544; e-mail: spinware@attmail.com.

Targeter's software database includes the names, titles, editorial interests, and phone and fax numbers of print and broadcast media contacts in the U.S. and Canada, as well as members of Congress and their staffs. Media Distribution Services, 307 West 36th Street, New York, New York 10018-6496. Tel: (212) 279-4800; Fax: (212) 714-9092.

Appendix C

Glossary

AAs — Changes made in copy by the writer or editor after the manuscript has been set in type. A percentage of the original cost of composition, usually 10 to 15 percent, is allowed the author for corrections, after which the compositor charges to make this type of correction.

access provider — Also called service providers. An organization that provides individuals or other organizations with access to the Internet.

actualities — Interviews conducted over the phone for use in radio news programming. The playback of such an interview usually is preceded by a beeping sound. See *radio beepers*.

affiliate — An independently owned radio or television station that airs or broadcasts a contractually agreed upon amount of network programming.

author's alterations — See *AAs*.

A wire — The national wire at any of the major wire services (i.e., the Associated Press, United Press International, and Reuters).

ballop card — A photo mounted on a piece of cardboard that is used as a visual aid in a television broadcast.

bleed — An illustration that extends to the edge of the page after the page has been trimmed.

bluelines — Also called *blueprints, blues,* or *plate proofs.* Photographic prints of typeset copy and/or artwork made for offset reproduction. As the last stage of proof before the material in question goes to press, blues merit special attention.

boards — Large sheets of stiff paper or specially coated cardboard on which the actual trim size of a book or brochure has been drawn in nonreproducing blue ink. Boards are used in the creation of dummies and mechanicals.

B roll — Sound bites recorded on a separate tape and sent along as accompaniment for a videotaped news story. Used by television stations when editing stories for broadcast.

browser — A software program that provides access to Web documents and allows them to be displayed on the user's computer screen.

B wire — The state wires at any of the major wire services (i.e., the Associated Press and United Press International). See *A wire.*

camera-ready copy — The final page proofs prepared by the compositor, usually in the form of reproductive proofs, or *repro.* Used to make the plates needed for offset printing.

clip — An article clipped from a newspaper or magazine. In radio and television, a clip (at least 10 words or more) is an audiotape or videotape of broadcast coverage.

clip art — Preprinted illustrations in sheet or book form. Increasingly available in a digitized format on CD-ROMs and at various sites on the World Wide Web.

color separation — The separation of a full-color transparency or print by photographing it with four color filters—process blue, process yellow, process red (magenta), and black. In a color separation, each of the four colors appears on an individual sheet of clear acetate. When placed over each other, the acetates combine to create the full-color image.

contingency line — An amount set aside in a budget to cover unanticipated expenses, escalating costs, and miscalculations.

crisis committee — A committee comprised of an organization's CEO, legal counsel, public relations director, outside public relations counsel (if retained), and chairperson. In the event of a crisis, the committee's job is to act as a "voice" for the organization, to deal with various constituents and stakeholders, and to set policy procedures.

cutline — A caption for a photograph.

daybook — A daily listing compiled and maintained by wire services in some cities of news conferences, upcoming events, and special programs.

double trucks — Print advertising positioned on facing pages (but not the center spread).

drop-in ads — Small advertisements, usually involving nothing more than an organization's name, logo, and slogan, used by magazines and newspapers as filler.

dummy — The preliminary pasteup of a book or brochure showing the position of copy, headings, subheads, captions, and illustrations and artwork in relation to each other. See *layout*.

duotone — A process for producing two-color illustrations in which two halftones of the same image, one in black-and-white and the other in a color, are printed together in register.

em — In printing, a unit of measurement equal to the space taken up by the letter *M* in a given font. In this glossary, the dashes separating words from their definitions are em dashes.

en — In printing, a unit of measurement equal to half an *em*.

exclusive — In public relations, a promise to a media outlet that it can run a story provided to it before anyone else.

external audience — A targeted group independent of an organization to which a specific organizational message is communicated.

F&Gs — Sheets from the press run that have been folded into signatures and "gathered" into the correct order for binding.

feed — A broadcast transmitted from a central source to various outlets.

field — A category of information in a database.

folio — A page number.

font — An assortment of type in a fixed size and face.

galley proofs — Also called *galleys*. The first proof of typeset copy. Galleys are usually sent to the author and a proofreader for proofreading, while a third set is used by the designer to mock up pages.

gutter — After a book is bound, the inside margins of facing pages.

grabber — A catchy phrase, anecdote, quote, or joke that grabs an audience's attention at the beginning of a speech.

halftone — A process in which a black-and-white photograph is rephotographed through a screen so that the gradations of light and dark in the original are converted into a pattern of tiny dots on a plate that print as a continuous tone.

head shot — A photograph of a person's head and shoulders.

home page — The opening document encountered by first-time visitors to any Web site. An effective home page works like a combination calling card and table of contents.

independent — A radio or television station not affiliated with a network.

internal audience — Any group within an organization, including but not necessarily limited to the staff and board, to which a specific organizational message is communicated.

Internet — A worldwide assemblage of computer networks; sometimes referred to as "the Information Superhighway." Used with the definite article, as in "the Internet."

issue kit — A kit containing printed background materials on issues that are important to an organization. Issue kits should be designed to outline and shape these issues for the media.

layout — The preliminary design of a book or brochure, including such elements as trim size, typeface, and the position of copy, headings, subheads, captions, and illustrations and artwork in relation to each other. See *dummy.*

lead — The opening paragraph of a story or news release.

leading — The space between typeset lines of copy.

line art — Rules, images, or other graphic elements that don't need to be screened in order to be reproduced.

lineup — The order in which stories are presented in a newscast.

live copy — Most often, a public-service announcement script that's distributed to radio stations (and, in some cases, television stations) and from which an announcer reads live.

mats — Camera-ready copy of news or feature releases that are produced and distributed to newspapers (usually local or suburban).

mechanical — A carefully prepared layout on a specially coated board showing the exact placement of all type and graphic elements. Used as camera-ready copy by the printer. See *camera-ready copy.*

mock-up — A designer's initial sketch or layout for a printed piece. See *dummy.*

modem — an acronym for modulator/demodulator. A piece of hardware that converts the analag forms used to transmit voice and data over phone wires into the digital forms used by computers, and vice versa.

offset lithography — A printing process that uses a photo-mechanical process to create an image on a plate that, when mounted on a cylinder, transfers ink to paper, reproducing the image.

pasteup — The process by which typeset copy and space for graphic elements are applied to a specially coated board to create a mechanical. Used as a noun, a *pasteup* is a mechanical.

PEs — An abbreviation for the errors introduced into galleys or page proofs by a compositor; in most instances, the compositor bears the cost of correcting PEs.

pica — A printer's unit of measure equal to 12 points, or about $\frac{1}{6}$ of an inch.

plate — A sheet of metal, plastic, rubber, or other material that, through one of various processes, is converted into a surface with a reproducible image on it.

plate proofs — See *bluelines.*

point — The basic typographical unit of measurement, equal to roughly $\frac{1}{72}$ of an inch; 12 points equals a pica.

premium — A specialty publication or other item (e.g., tote bags, umbrellas, coffee mugs, etc.) produced by an organization at its own expense and offered to a specific audience as an inducement.

press sheets — See *F&Gs.*

printer's errors — See *PEs.*

PSAs — A precisely timed message for radio or television broadcast that addresses an issue of concern to the general public.

public-service announcements — See *PSAs.*

radio beepers — Interviews conducted over the phone for use in radio programming. The playback of such an interview usually is preceded by a beeping sound. See *actualities.*

register — In four-color printing, the printing of each screen of an image in the correct position in relation to other screens of the same image in order to create a clear, undistorted final image. If any of the four screens is not aligned properly, the image is said to be *out of register.*

reminder mailing — A mailing sent to reporters and editors just prior to a media event in order to encourage attendance at the event.

reproduction proofs — Also called *repro.* Final proofs intended to be used as camera-ready copy.

rough cut — The first edit of a filmed piece, before sound and titles have been added.

screen — In order to print a photograph, its gray tones must be translated into a pattern of solid dots. The larger the dots, the coarser the screen. Typically, newspapers use a screen that has approximately 65 dots per square inch. The fine screens used for reproductions in magazines and art books generally have 110+ dots per square inch.

separation — See *color separation.*

service-oriented news release — News releases that, instead of publicizing some aspect of an organization, provide timely information about an issue of interest to the general public.

signature — A sheet of paper folded so that, when cut, it will produce a certain number of pages (usually 32, but any multiple of four is acceptable).

specs — Instructions for a compositor regarding type size, style, and leading.

simulcast — A simultaneous broadcast over radio and television stations.

stat — Short for *photostat*. A reproducible image on acetate of text or line art.

storyboard — A panel or panels on which a sequence of sketches depict the significant changes of action in a planned film or presentation.

stringer — A part-time correspondent covering his or her local area for a wire service or newspaper published elsewhere.

talking head — Used as a noun, it refers to an on-camera personality in television news programming (because that person is usually shown from the shoulders up). As an adjective, it refers to a program format in which two or more people sit in a studio and discuss a predetermined agenda.

trade media — The various professional and specialty print and electronic media outlets that deal with specific industries and interests.

trim size — The size of the final printed piece after the pages have been trimmed.

URL (uniform resource locator) — The "address" assigned to every document on the Web. URLs consist of the domain name of the Web server (computer) where a document resides, the port address of that server, and the directory path leading to the document in question.

video news release (VNR) — A videotaped news segment, usually three to five minutes in length, that is produced and distributed to television stations around the country for broadcast in local news programs.

voiceover — An audio track, usually comprised of explanatory narration, added to film, video, or slide presentations.

Web site — A set of addressed Web pages to which access is provided by a Web server. See *home page*.

World Wide Web — Also called "WWW," "W3," or, simply, "the Web." An interactive global computer network whose graphical interface and hypertext capabilities have made it the fastest-growing segment of the Internet.

Appendix D

Public Relations Bibliography

Aronson, Merry, and Don Spetner. *The Public Relations Writer's Handbook*. New York: Lexington Books, 1993.

Beach, Mark. *Editing Your Newsletter*. Third edition. Manzanita, Oregon: Coast to Coast Books, 1988.

Bianco, David, editor. *PR News Casebook*. Detroit: Gale Research Inc., 1993.

Braun, Eric. *The Internet Directory*. New York: Fawcett Columbine/Ballantine Books, 1993.

Brody, E.W., and Dan L. Lattimore. *Public Relations Writing*. Westport, Connecticut: Greenwood Publishing Group, 1990.

Burlingame, Dwight, and Lamont Hulse. *Taking Fund Raising Seriously*. San Francisco: Jossey-Bass Inc. Publishing, 1991.

Cappon, Rene. *The Word—An AP Guide to Good News Writing.* New York: Associated Press, 1992.

Chambers, Wicke, and Spring Asher. *TV PR: How to Promote Yourself, Your Product, Your Service or Your Organization on TV.* Roseville, California: Prima Publishing, 1987.

CTS, various editors. *Selecting Software for NonProfit Organizations and Trade Associations.* Rockville, Maryland: Computer Training Service, 1994.

Connors, Tracy. *Nonprofit Organization Handbook.* Second edition. New York: McGraw-Hill Inc., 1988.

Dern, Daniel. *The Internet Guide for New Users.* New York: McGraw-Hill Inc., 1993.

Eckhardt, Robert, et al. *Desktop Publishing Secrets.* Berkeley: Peachpit Press, 1992.

Engst, Adam C. *The Internet Starter Kit: Everything You Need to Get on the Internet.* Indianapolis: Hayden Books, 1994.

Ernst & Young Staff. *The Complete Guide to Special Events Management.* New York: John Wiley & Sons Inc., 1992.

Espy, Siri. *Marketing for Nonprofit Organizations.* Chicago: Lyceum Books, 1992.

Felici, James, and Ted Nace. *Desktop Publishing Skills.* Redding, Massachusetts: Addison-Wesley Pubishing Company, 1987.

Harris, April. *Special Events: Planning for Success.* Washington, D.C.: CASE Publishing, 1988.

Hudson, Howard Penn. *Publishing Newsletters.* New York: Macmillan Publishing, 1988.

Jacobi, Peter. *Writing with Style: The News Story and the Feature.* Chicago: Ragan Communications, 1982.

Kennedy, Larry. *Quality Management in the Nonprofit World.* San Francisco: Jossey-Bass Inc. Publishing, 1991.

Klepper, Michael M. *I'd Rather Die Than Give a Speech*. Ridge, Illinois: Irwin Professional Publishing, 1994.

Kotler, Philip, and Alan Andreason. *Strategic Marketing for Nonprofit Organizations*. New York: Prentice-Hall Publishing, 1987.

Lesly, Philip. *Lesly's Handbook of Public Relations and Communications*. Chicago: Probus Publishing, 1990.

Levine, Michael. *Guerrilla PR: How You Can Wage an Effective Publicity Campaign Without Going Broke*. New York: HarperCollins Publishers, 1993.

Lord, James G. *Philanthropy and Marketing: New Strategies for Fund Raising*. Cleveland: Third Sector Press, 1981.

Newsom, Doug, Alan Scott, and Judy VanSlyke. *This is PR*. Fifth edition. Belmont, California: Wadsworth Publishing Company, 1993.

Newsom, Doug, and Bob Carrell. *Public Relations Writing: Form and Style*. Third edition. Belmont, California: Wadsworth Publishing, 1991.

Rados, David. *Marketing for Nonprofit Organizations*. Westport, Connecticut: Greenwood Publishing Group, 1981.

Rosso, Henry. *Achieving Excellence in Fund Raising*. San Francisco: Jossey-Bass Inc. Publishing, 1991.

St. John, Tracy. *Getting Your Public Relations Story on TV & Radio*. Babylon, New York: Pilot Books, 1986.

Seitel, Fraser P. *The Practice of Public Relations*. Fifth edition. New York: Macmillan Publishing, 1992.

Stopler, Carolyn, and Karen Hopkins. *Successful Fundraising for Arts & Cultural Organizations*. Phoenix: Oryx Press, 1989.

Tucker, Kerry, and Doris Derelian. *Public Relations Writing*. New York: Prentice-Hall Publishing, 1989.

Wales, La Rae. *Practical Guide to Newsletter Editing/Design*. Second edition. Ann Arbor: Books on Demand, 1976.

Walsh, Frank. *Public Relations Writer in a Computer Age.* New York: Prentice-Hall Publishing, 1986.

Wolff, Michael, et al. *Netguide.* New York: Random House, 1994.

Wragg, David. *Targeting Media Relations: A Step-by-Step Guide to Cost Effective Public Relations.* Portland, Oregon: Kogan Page Limited, 1993.

Yale, David. *The Publicity Handbook.* Lincolnwood, Illinois: NTC Business, 1991.

Index